The Jessie and John Danz Lectures

The Jessie and John Danz Lectures

The Human Crisis, by Julian Huxley
Of Men and Galaxies, by Fred Hoyle
The Challenge of Science, by George Boas
Of Molecules and Men, by Francis Crick
Nothing But or Something More, by Jacquetta Hawkes
How Musical Is Man?, by John Blacking
*Abortion in a Crowded World: The Problem of Abortion
    with Special Reference to India*, by S. Chandrasekhar
World Culture and the Black Experience, by Ali Mazrui
Energy for Tomorrow, by Philip H. Abelson
Plato's Universe, by Gregory Vlastos
The Nature of Biography, by Robert Gittings
Darwinism and Human Affairs, by Richard D. Alexander
Arms Control and SALT II, by W. K. H. Panofsky
*Promethean Ethics: Living with Death, Competition,
    and Triage*, by Garrett Hardin
Social Environment and Health, by Stewart Wolf
The Possible and the Actual, by François Jacob
Facing the Threat of Nuclear Weapons, by Sidney D. Drell
Symmetries, Asymmetries, and the World of Particles,
    by T. D. Lee
*The Symbolism of Habitat: An Interpretation of Landscape
    in the Arts*, by Jay Appleton
The Essence of Chaos, by Edward N. Lorenz
*Environmental Health Risks and Public Policy:
    Decision Making in Free Societies*, by David V. Bates
Language and Human Behavior, by Derek Bickerton

Language
and
human
behavior

Derek Bickerton

UNIVERSITY OF WASHINGTON PRESS
Seattle

Copyright © 1995 by the University of Washington Press
Printed in the United States of America

Language and Human Behaviour is published in the United Kingdom by UCL Press
Limited, University Collge, London

Library of Congress Cataloging-in-Publication Data

Bickerton, Derek.
    Language and human behavior / Derek Bickerton.
      p.   cm. —(The Jessie and John Danz lectures)
    Includes bibliographical references (p.) and index.
    ISBN 0-295-97457-5 (cloth : alk. paper).
    1. Language and languages.   2. Human evolution   3. Psycholinguistics.
    I. Title   II. Series.
    P106.B467   1995
    400—dc20   95-17023
                                                  CIP

The paper used in this publication meets the minimum requirements of American
National Standard for Information Sciences—Permanence of Paper for Printed
Library Materials, ANSI Z39.48-1984. ◉ ∞

The Jessie and John Danz Lectures

In October 1961, Mr. John Danz, a Seattle pioneer, and his wife, Jessie Danz, made a substantial gift to the University of Washington to establish a perpetual fund to provide income to be used to bring to the University of Washington each year "distinguished scholars of national and international reputation who have concerned themselves with the impact of science and philosophy on man's perception of a rational universe." The fund established by Mr. and Mrs. Danz is now known as the Jessie and John Danz Fund, and the scholars brought to the University under its provisions are known as Jessie and John Danz Lecturers or Professors.

Mr. Danz wisely left to the Board of Regents of the University of Washington the identification of the special fields in science, philosophy, and other disciplines in which lectureships may be established. His major concern and interest were that the fund would enable the University of Washington to bring to the campus some of the truly great scholars and thinkers of the world.

Mr. Danz authorized the Regents to expend a portion of the income from the fund to purchase special collections of books, documents, and other scholarly materials needed to reinforce the effectiveness of the extraordinary lectureships and professorships. The terms of the gift also provided for the publication and dissemination, when this seems appropriate, of the lectures given by the Jessie and John Danz Lecturers.

Through this book, therefore, another Jessie and John Danz Lecturer speaks to the people and scholars of the world, as he has spoken to his audiences at the University of Washington and in the Pacific Northwest community.

Contents

ACKNOWLEDGMENTS

I wish to express my gratitude to Frederick J. Newmeyer and the Jessie and John Danz Lectureship Committee of the University of Washington for inviting me to present three public lectures in Seattle in October 1992 and encouraging me to expand those lectures into the present book.

I deeply appreciate the continued support of the Linguistics Department and the Social Sciences Research Institute of the University of Hawaii, which have enabled me to pursue my researches with the minimum of interference from other responsibilities.

I am particularly grateful to William Calvin, Noam Chomsky, Daniel Dennett, and Steven Pinker for reading and commenting on sections of the manuscript and to three anonymous reviewers, one of whom was Ray Jackendoff, for their comments on the manuscript as a whole. All of their remarks helped enormously in making this a better book, and where I have willfully chosen to ignore their good advice, I alone am to blame.

As for the contribution of my wife Yvonne, I shall say nothing, since no words of mine could adequately convey the depth or the breadth of my indebtedness to her.

Language and human behavior

Introduction

The material on which this book is based was first presented in three public lectures at the University of Washington under the sponsorship of the Jessie and John Danz Fund. In inaugurating the Danz lecture series, the principal motive of its founder and benefactor John Danz was to bring to the university scholars who had "concerned themselves with the impact of science and philosophy on man's perception of a rational universe." When Danz spoke of a "rational universe," what did he have in mind? Surely no more (and no less!) than a universe that is lawful, about which we can make significant generalizations that hold over broad domains, and in which, if one selects an appropriate level of abstraction, the purely contingent has no role to play.

Assumptions of this nature are routinely made in the physical sciences—made without needing to be stated—for no science is possible otherwise. But those assumptions are not always made, or held to, in the behavioral sciences. When humans study themselves, they often hold the view that different rules apply, or that they are somehow exempt from the lawfulness that governs other forms of matter.

I feel that John Danz would have rejected such a view, and would have been absolutely right to do so. And yet one has to admit that those sciences that have tried to account rationally for human behavior have come nowhere near equaling the achievements of the physical sciences. The physical sciences have given us penetrating insights into the nature of matter and have even dared to suggest how matter came into existence. They have done a much better job of describing the material universe than literature has. Yet despite much effort on the part of the behavioral sciences, we still, in words cited approvingly by a previous Danz lecturer (Alexander 1979:ix), "don't know who we are, or where we came from, or what we have done, or why." If we want to obtain a glimmering of what human nature is like, we are still on firmer ground with Shakespeare or Aeschylus or Joyce or Dostoyevsky than with any behavioral scientist.

There is a more concrete dimension to this contrast. While the link between theoretical concepts and practical achievements is by no means always as tight as it appears, such achievements do give a sense of confidence that the theories supporting them must be heading in the right direction. The physical sciences can show an abundance of this kind

3

of support: thanks to their discoveries we can communicate instantly around the globe, circumnavigate it in a matter of hours, even leave it altogether for longer and longer periods.

Compared to this, how dismal is our record in the behavioral domain! It would be bad enough to have to confess that most problems of human behavior are never solved, despite the myriad solutions proposed for them. It is worse to have to admit that many of those problems, far from being ameliorated, become more and more intractable with the passage of time. As our physical control over matter tightens, our ability to control ourselves seems to diminish. Economists can't predict slumps, sociologists can't prevent or even explain burgeoning crime and drug abuse, psychiatrists can't cure patients any faster than time, unaided, can do the job, and the unending cycles of famine, destitution, injustice, and violence continue to repeat themselves, intensified rather than diminished despite recent claims of an imminent "end of history."

Alibis are, of course, continually being offered. The behavioral sciences have not been around as long as the physical sciences (but that shouldn't matter, since most of the scientists who ever lived are living now). Humans are more difficult to investigate than matter (but the only tangible evidence for this is precisely that failure to achieve results which constitutes the datum to be explained!). Worst of all alibis, humans are perceived as something special, intrinsically unknowable, having somehow fallen outside the envelope of lawfulness that embraces everything else. Human culture, we are sometimes told, has liberated us from biological constraints; we are free to become gods, if we choose (Stenger 1988). We can do anything and everything except explain what we are and why we are what we are, for that cannot be explained— what we are is simply what we choose to be. Those who assure us of such things seldom draw the obvious conclusion: if what they say were true, we would be faced with the bizarre paradox that so-called rational beings represent the only element of unreason in an otherwise rational universe![1]

Small wonder that some have fled to the opposite extreme and claimed that laws applicable to other species exhaustively account for human behavior. The sociobiologists who have spearheaded this movement have

1. For an insightful discussion of some approaches that place humans above natural law, see Midgley (1985).

not been cautious in their predictions of what such an approach might achieve: according to Edward Wilson (1975:574–75), by the end of the twenty-first century, "biology should be at its peak, with the social sciences maturing rapidly. . . . Having cannibalized psychology, the new neurobiology will yield an enduring set of first principles for sociology. . . . Skinner's dream of a culture predesigned for happiness will surely have to wait for the new neurobiology." Essentially the sociobiological program for studying human behavior involves taking the biological imperatives that govern animals in general, showing how those imperatives continue to manifest themselves in our species despite the sometimes camouflaging effects of culture, and (hopefully) then demonstrating the neurological bases of the behaviors that result. In the words of a recent attempt to execute this program (Ridley 1993:4), "there is nothing in our natures that was not carefully 'chosen' . . . for its ability to contribute to eventual reproductive success."

It is perhaps not unfair to say that this approach can tell us all we need to know about the least interesting aspects of human behavior. For surely what is most interesting about human behavior (certainly the most essential, if we are to understand our true nature, and our relationship with the rest of nature) is precisely the part of it that we do *not* share with other creatures. Indeed, the core of the whole problem of human nature lies in the following paradox: humans are a species produced like all other species by the natural workings of biological evolution, yet the behavior of humans differs dramatically from that of all other species over a wide variety of parameters.

It is fashionable in some circles to deny this, to claim that we are just another species, that our uniqueness merely reflects the fact that all species are unique.[2] Attitudes of such apparent modesty tend to receive approval when contrasted with the "crown of creation/masters of the universe" bombast common earlier this century (and not entirely extinguished); indeed, it is to precisely such bombast that the "just another species" gambit forms an understandable reaction. But that gambit looks somewhat less attractive in the context of the present plight of nature. What other "unique species" has already decimated the global ecology and threatens to remove 25 to 30 percent of existing species within the

2. The title "Another Unique Species" was used for what is in fact one of the more illuminating recent studies in paleoanthropology (Foley 1987).

next few decades if left unchecked? (Wilson 1992). What other "unique species" stands ready to contaminate other planets with its unique peculiarities? For better or worse (and you may well conclude for worse) our species possesses not merely powers many orders of magnitude greater than those of other creatures, but powers that differ radically *in kind*— powers wholly without precedent in the evolutionary history of earth. In these circumstances, to persist in claiming that we are just another species is not just hypocrisy: it is irresponsibility.

Moreover, the claim that we are just another species ignores the range as well as the power of human behavior. The range of behavior in other creatures does not extend much beyond seeking food, seeking sex, rearing and protecting young, resisting predation, grooming, fighting rivals, exploring and defending territory, and unstructured play. Human beings do all of these things, of course, but they also do math, tap dance, engage in commerce, build boats, play chess, invent novel artifacts, drive vehicles, litigate, draw representationally, and do countless other things that no other species ever did. Any theory that would account for human behavior has to explain why the behavior of all other species is, relatively speaking, so limited, while that of one single species should be so broad. Why is there not a continuum of behaviors, growing gradually from amoeba to human? Why don't chimpanzees build boats, why can't orangutans tap dance?

No extant theory of human behavior can explain these anomalies. Even when they are acknowledged, the things that mark us off from other species are renamed, rather than explained. Our distinctive features are said to result from our great intelligence, our unique cognitive capacities, our consciousness, the complexity of our brains, and so on and so forth. This is like saying our water glass is full because there's a lot of H_2O in it. How did we achieve our level of intelligence, how did we arrive at consciousness, what made our brains so complex, and why should that complexity endow us with consciousness, intelligence, and unprecedented power over nature? Why should our behavior differ from that of other species in so many ways? We cannot provide satisfactory answers for any of these questions. We lack even a basic understanding of the most fundamental factors that make a human being human.

Suppose, however, that these deficiencies in the behavioral sciences stem not from the short time that those sciences have had to develop, nor from the difficulty of the problems they face, nor from the intrinsic lawlessness of human nature, nor from any of the other causes that have so far been suggested. Suppose that the behavioral sciences have failed to achieve their larger objectives simply because they started in the wrong places and made the wrong assumptions. Suppose that some single characteristic of humans turns out to be the antecedent of most or even all of the other characteristics that differentiate us even from our closest relatives among the apes. If this were so, the reasons for the confusion I have described would be plain enough. We would have failed to provide an adequate explanation of our species simply because we tried to examine each of that species' distinctive attributes as if they were separate and wholly unrelated traits, rather than logical entailments of some single determining capacity.

In this book, language is proposed as just such a capacity. The first chapter examines language and its defining properties, distinguishing them from other forms of communication and indicating their most probable source. The second chapter shows how the capacity for language evolved as the end product of tendencies long latent in what are sometimes termed "more advanced" creatures, and how by the very nature of its evolution language created the ground on which subsequent mental developments could (perhaps had to) arise. The third chapter proposes that the peculiar properties of a distinctively human intelligence are such as derive straightforwardly from the possession of language. Finally, the fourth chapter suggests that consciousness as we know it may arise from an identical source.

Such a program will undoubtedly meet with resistance. Some may well dismiss it as reductionist, forgetting that most improvements in our understanding of nature have come about through some form of reductionism. But reductionism has become a dirty word in the context of the human species. Like some wealthy patient of a Viennese psychiatrist at the turn of the last century, we feel flattered by the thought that we are really very complex creatures, with layer upon layer of fascinating mystery surrounding us—mystery that requires patient unraveling in an awed hush of self-reverence.

Some may even fear that to reduce our specialness to a single attribute might demean us, even license a more contemptuous attitude to humans and their creations than has hitherto existed. After all, if we are merely apes that happen to be able to talk, what are our achievements worth, what objective value can be placed on individual human lives? But if such fears exist, they are surely misplaced. The concepts of human superiority current over the last couple of centuries did not prevent the extermination of Jews and Gypsies in Germany, of kulaks in the Soviet Union, or of indigenous peoples in the Americas and elsewhere. Indeed, anyone looking at conditions in the world today may well wonder how any change in our beliefs about ourselves could make matters worse than they are now.

In fact the era of the most wildly inflated beliefs in human supremacy has also been the era of the most cynical and egregious crimes against humanity. So striking is this coincidence, one is tempted to propose an exactly contrary theme: an inflated concept of human nature is precisely what licenses such crimes. For the justification of those crimes has always consisted in identifying the perpetrators as the true heirs to this miraculous human heritage, and the victims as subhuman obstacles to the perpetrators' purposes. Perhaps our conduct toward others of our own species (not to mention other species) might be improved rather than worsened by a little humility. Perhaps if we woke to find ourselves all together on the same low plateau, one bare and precarious step above the chimpanzee, some of this lethal vainglory might evaporate.

What might at first seem a more logical objection to the program proposed here lies in the belief, so widespread in the behavioral sciences, that language is simply a means of communication, one of the many skills that our huge brains have allowed us to master. So potent is this misconception, and so little combated by those professional linguists whose duty should be to challenge it at every turn, that it has seduced many of the best minds in a wide range of disciplines. For example, biologist J. Z. Young finds it "rather perverse not to consider human spoken or written language as primarily a functional system evolved for communication" (1978:175). Similarly, philosopher Patricia Churchland says: "Language is a social art, and linguistic behavior serves a communicative function" (1986:388). And in the same vein Eric Newell, leading theorist in computer science and artificial intelligence, opines: "[L]anguage is patently a skill. . . . A fortiori, language will be dealt with [in devising a model of human cognition, DB] from a functional standpoint. . . . It is easy enough to denote the overall function as communication" (1990:441). Such quotations could be multiplied ad nauseam.

If one envisages language as no more than a skill used to express and communicate the products of human thought, it becomes ipso facto impossible to regard language as the Rubicon that divides us from other species. A quite different scenario then seems inescapable—a scenario whose superficial plausibility has already endeared it to several generations in the behavioral sciences, and which is well summarized by Nadeau (1991:173): "The evolutionary success of our species is commonly expressed in terms of our larger brain size. . . . [B]rain size . . . became an evolutionary advantage at the point at which the excess neuronal capacity allowed us to invent a new tool. . . . *Homo habilis* may have been the first of our ancestors with enough excess neuronal organization, or hardware, to invent the first rudimentary elements of human language. . . . During the million-year transition from *Homo habilis* to *erectus*, the neocortex, which became the principal center for association and thought, more than doubled in size."

Paleoanthropologist Philip Tobias (1971:xi) put it rather more succinctly: "increase in brain size = gain in neuronal organization = rise in complexity of nervous function = even more diversified and complicated behavioral responses = progressively amplified and enhanced cultural manifestations." Or in other words, "Tools, hunting, fire, complex social life, speech, the human way and the brain evolved together to produce ancient man of the genus *Homo*" (Washburn 1960).

But this scenario and these equations are not just grossly simplistic. They run dead counter to the empirical data given us by the fossil record itself, the lithic bible on which all these exegeses are supposed to be based! Incredible though it must seem, some of the most salient and widely known facts about the course of development followed by our species are wholly at variance with such a view of things. How fact and interpretation in paleoanthropology have managed to remain disjoint is a question for future historians of science, and will not be broached in these pages. Documenting the existence of this still unacknowledged conflict, together with its nature and extent, will form a topic for the second chapter in this book.

Before that issue can be taken up, however, a more pressing concern must be dealt with. This is a book about language and the logical consequences of the possession of language, for any species (un?)fortunate enough to possess it. But such a book cannot hope to convince its readers unless it clearly sets forth exactly what language is (a task that linguists have very often been accused, not wholly without justice, of shirking). If language is not simply a skill or simply a means of communication, what exactly is it?

Chapter 1

What language is

The term *language* has been put to a variety of uses, or misuses. We hear about the language of flowers or body language; people speak of animal language or the language of bees.[1] Because so many people confuse language with communication, pretty well anything that communicates may be called a language. Such usages have contributed to a widespread misunderstanding of the role of language in human behavior.

The misunderstanding is twofold. First, there is the persistent confusion between a thing and the uses of a thing. This should not be a problem at all. People who blithely say "Language is (a form of) communication" do not confuse cars with driving, scissors with cutting, or forks with eating. If language were a visible tool that you physically used, the confusion could hardly arise. But language is more abstract than cars or scissors, and when thing and use are both abstract the absurdity of conflating them becomes less apparent. Given the object-use distinction, nonhuman communication systems are not communication, either. Nor, for that matter, are body language, the language of flowers, and so on. Like language, they are representational systems used for communication.

The second part of the misunderstanding arises because animal communication systems,[2] and all the other things illegitimately described as languages, differ from language in that they can do nothing *but* communicate. Language has additional capabilities, and subsequent chapters will show some of the ways it is used to store information or carry out thought processes.[3] These by no means exhaust its functions. But one

1. This abuse is not confined to the term *language* itself, but extends to the subcomponents of language. Thus, in a recent work on language and evolution (Gibson and Ingold 1993), we hear about "auditory syntactic capacities" and "the syntax of performance." It should be clear that hearing has nothing to do with syntax, and that to use "syntax" as a descriptor for any serial process simply deprives the term of any useful meaning.

2. Strictly speaking, I suppose one should say "nonhuman communication systems," since humans are, of course, animals. However, the term *animal communication system* is widely used and understood, and has the advantage that it excludes purely mechanical systems (traffic signals, systems incorporated in robots, and the like) which one would prefer to exclude.

3. This latter procedure has sometimes been pulled kicking and screaming under the communication blanket by the claim that thinking is communicating with

cannot think in body language, or use an animal communication system to store information. If something can be used for only one thing, it is easier to confuse use and thing. The unconscious thought process evolves as follows: animal communication systems are equated with communication, and then language is equated with animal communication systems. So by simple transitivity the solecism "language equals communication" gets committed.

What can different representational systems represent?

The fact that both language and animal communication systems are representational does not mean that they must be accepted as members of the same class. Even from the viewpoint of communication, they differ with respect to what they can communicate and how they communicate it.

Just what kinds of information can be conveyed by nonlinguistic systems? In what is known as *body language*, a person can convey interest in another by body posture, turning or leaning attentively before the object of attention; by direction and intensity of gaze; by spreading arms or legs in a gesture that signifies openness; and by a variety of other subtle means. Similarly, disinterest can be conveyed by a turning away of the body, a closure of the limbs, a dull or distracted gaze, and so on. But one cannot, in this medium, indicate one's profession, one's income, one's interests, or one's taste in wine. This so-called language can convey information about states, conditions, or feelings, but cannot convey much in the way of factual information about objective features of the world.

Interestingly enough, *body language* as used by humans suffers the same limitations as "*animal languages.*" The latter, with few apparent exceptions, and perhaps no real exceptions, similarly indicate how the animal feels or what the animal wants, but not what the animal knows. Most if not all of these systems have a narrow range of topics: willingness (or otherwise) to mate, willingness (or otherwise) to defend territory, aggression or appeasement directed toward a conspecific, maintenance

---

oneself! Which fragment of oneself might be communicating with which other fragment is just one of the pseudoquestions which, hopefully, Chapter 4 will dissolve.

of contact with other members of one's group, or alarm calls that warn of the approach of predators.

Alarm calls might, at first blush, be regarded as utterances that convey factual, objective information—"Here comes a predator!"—or even (in more sophisticated species like vervet monkeys) as protowords for the kind of predator to which they are a response. But problems with the concept of meaning make it difficult to know how to interpret alarm calls. There is a world of difference between inferred meaning and intended meaning: between "That cloud means rain" and "The words 'kindly leave' mean 'get the hell out.'" If I say "Kindly leave" then I want you to get out, and I intend you to know that I want you to get out. But the cloud neither wants to rain nor intends you to know that it is going to rain. The use of the word "mean" in both contexts blurs the distinction between a meaning that can be inferred by an observer and a meaning that is intended by an agent (and can, hopefully, be interpreted in the same sense by a recipient). The fact that the second proviso may be lacking emphasizes the difference between these two meanings of "meaning." The cloud can "mean" only if it has an observer, but I can mean in the complete absence of anyone who comprehends my meaning.

So it may well be a mistake to think that a warning cry actually *means* (in the human sense of meaning) "There is a predator approaching." It might simply mean "I am alarmed by a predator approaching." If that were so, then the warning call would be just another case of how-I'm-feeling-right-now. And of course, "I am alarmed by a predator approaching" logically entails "There is a predator approaching."

But this might suggest that animal calls are merely reflex responses, like our own start of surprise at a sudden loud noise. In fact, things turn out to be slightly more complex than that. Cheney and Seyfarth (1990, chap. 5) have shown conclusively that vervet monkeys (along with other species) do not always call when a predator appears, and that the likelihood of their calling will be influenced by contextual factors, such as the presence or absence of close kin. A better or at least a fuller paraphrase might be "I am alarmed by a predator approaching and I feel you should share my alarm." This still would lie firmly within the domain of what-I-feel-or-want rather than what-I-know.

Cheney and Seyfarth themselves go somewhat further, claiming that "monkeys give leopard alarms because they want others to run into trees" (1990:174). They may be right, but it would not be easy (even for Cheney and Seyfarth, who are old hands at designing ingenious experiments) to design an experiment that would tease apart the meaning they propose from the meaning "I am alarmed by a terrestrial predator and you too should be alarmed." For, given that running up trees is the preferred vervet strategy for avoiding terrestrial predators, and that an isolated vervet, faced with such a predator, will give no alarm call but will run up a tree, we can assume that running up a tree is no more than a response to the presence (whether personally observed or inferred from a call) of a terrestrial predator, and thus one which would occur whether the warning monkey wanted it to or not. The more parsimonious assumption is that only the animal's own state or condition is being conveyed. And in any case, even what-I-want is still very far from what-I-know.

Does the fact that monkeys occasionally give alarm calls when no predator is present constitute evidence for a less parsimonious interpretation? There is considerable if largely anecdotal evidence (see Whiten and Byrne 1988, Byrne and Whiten 1988) to indicate that monkeys will give such calls when they are being attacked by other monkeys or when they wish to keep some tasty morsel of food for themselves. However, there is no indication here that an alarm-sounding monkey specifically wants other monkeys to run up trees. The alarm-sounding monkey merely wants all other monkeys out of its immediate vicinity; its own observations will have sufficed to show it that alarm calls do remove all monkeys from the immediate vicinity of the caller. All we have to assume for this behavior is some degree of volitional control over calling; and we already know that vervets have such control from the fact that they respond differently in the presence or absence of kin.

Thus one cannot conclude that the alarm calls of vervets (or of any other species) convey factual information, even though information may be inferred from them. On the contrary, animal communication systems convey the current state of the sender or try to manipulate the behavior of the receiver. Human language, on the other hand, is not restricted to expressing an individual's wants or feelings, nor to manipulation, although it can and frequently does serve these purposes. It can also convey an infinite amount of information: not just things like phone numbers, professions, or tastes in music or wine, but the (actual) size of the earth, the (estimated) age of the universe, the basic principles of marketing or mathematics, the habits of the scarab beetle, the behavior of protons, the events that took place in Madrid on May 2, 1808—things that have only the most indirect and tenuous connection, if any, with what the speaker or writer immediately wants or feels.

There might seem to be at least one exception to the generalizations made above about animal communication systems. One such system—that of bees (von Frisch 1967)—does carry factual information regarding direction, distance, and quality of food supplies. However, bees cannot convey any other information, and even information about food is far from complete. When one of von Frisch's assistants placed a food supply in a tower, the bees that found it failed completely in their attempts to explain its whereabouts to colleagues. Bee "space," or rather the kind of space that can be represented in the bee communication systems, is two-dimensional: bees can indicate horizontal but not vertical directions and distances. Now there may be dimensions in the universe about which we cannot speak; but, unlike bees, we can speak about all the dimensions we experience, and even a few that we don't.

It might seem, however, as if bees do breach one limit that otherwise constrains all animal systems: an inability to communicate about anything occurring in the past, the future, or any place other than where sender and receiver currently find themselves. Bee messages refer to objects at some distance from the hive at which those messages are delivered; one might even claim that they refer to events (discoveries of food sources) that are already in the past when the message is given. But these messages are limited to the most recent of such incidents. There is no way a bee can compare the richness of its latest find with that of the source it discovered yesterday, or express a hope that it may find a still richer source tomorrow. Similarly it cannot state that today's source is twice as far from the hive as yesterday's, or some distance to the east of it. The capacity to refer to a past event or a remote place does not entail the complete freedom of movement in time and space that language bestows.

For language, of course, knows no limitations of space or time. Even when merely conveying our wants, needs, and feelings, it does so in a much more sophisticated way than animal communication systems do. Although it is hard to prove, most animals appear to be on the level of what Dennett (1987) would call "first-order intentionality": they have states of mind, but do not necessarily make inferences about the state of mind of others, or even know that others can have states of mind different from their own (see Premack 1985 for a comparison of chimpanzees with human children in this respect).[4] Humans, on the other hand, can reach dizzying levels of third- or even higher-order intentionality, being able to say or think things like "I want X to think that I want him to run up a tree because he is a contrary fellow and if he thinks I want him to run up a tree he won't, which is what I really want."

As regards the quantity or the complexity of information that can be conveyed, there is simply no contest between human language and other so-called languages. One might claim that if humans are the most complex creatures, the fact that they have the most complex communication system can hardly be unexpected. But while this is true, it fails to account for the absolute discontinuity between humans and other species. What you would expect, if mere complexity were at issue, would be some kind of gradual increase in the number of things that animals could communicate about, starting with very few among the simpler organisms and finishing with very many (almost as many as we can communicate about, perhaps) among our nearest relatives, the apes. In fact, as Edward Wilson (1972) has shown, there is little difference in the richness of communication systems over a wide range of fish, birds, and mammals (see Table 1.1). All other creatures stand on the same low plateau; we alone tower above it.

This is not just a matter of numerical superiority. Language is an open system, while animal communication systems are closed. By this I mean that no matter how many things we can talk about, we can always add new things. Animal systems are not absolutely impervious to change: the work of Cheney and Seyfarth cited above shows, for instance, that the call repertoire of vervets varies in different parts of Africa, and thus has obviously been added to or changed. But the few changes that do take place do so with the glacial slowness of biological evolution, whereas

4. The higher primates may be exceptions to this particular generalization. Whiten and Byrne (1988) recount numerous cases which suggest this, and indeed the conclusion is hard to escape in cases like the following: chimpanzee A, on seeing larger and more aggressive chimpanzee B approach, nonchalantly closes the lid of a box containing food and saunters away, returning only when B disappears. But B, lurking behind a tree, peeps out and sees A reopen the box, whereupon B grabs the food from A!

Table 1.1

Number of units in the communication systems of fish, birds, and mammals

Fish		Birds		Mammals	
Bullhead	10				
Stickleback	11				
Guppy	15	Sparrow	15		
Sunfish	15				
				*Night monkey	16
				Deer mouse	16
		Great tit	17	Coati	17
		Kingbird	18	Prairie dog	18
		Skua	18		
		Mallard	19		
Mouthbreeder	21	Sparrow	21	*Sifaka	21
				Zebra	23
				*Patas monkey	24
		Chaffinch	25	Grant's gazelle	25
		Coot	25	Polecat	25
Badis	26	Green heron	26	Elk	26
				*Dusky titi	27
		Hooded gull	28		
				*Tamarin	32
				*Ring-tailed lemur	34
				*Rhesus monkey	37

*Indicates primates.
Data from Wilson (1972), Figures 1.6, 1.7, and 1.8.

humans are constantly thinking of new things to talk about: things like sound bites or carjacking that were unheard-of a few years ago. The fact that we can add freely to our list of topics, while other species cannot, indicates a difference in kind, not in degree.

The role of symbolism in communication

One might claim that language shares with other "languages" the use of symbols to convey meaning. But here again there are both quantitative and qualitative differences. The symbols used in animal communication are largely *iconic*: the relation between the message expressed and the form of expressing it is straightforward and transparent. Lowering the head and/or gaze or presentation of the rump may indicate submission, while expansion of body size by inhaling air or extending hair or feathers may indicate aggression and intention to dominate. However, a reverse relationship between affect and representation (e.g., gaze lowering or rump presentation to signal dominance, expansion of body size to signal submission) is never found. Even among sounds, we find widespread consistencies. Across a wide range of species, according to Morton and Page (1991), high-pitched, squeaky sounds indicate submission, while deep, rasping sounds indicate dominance. There are, of course, exceptions, though the reverse relationship seems nonexistent.

But there is at least one apparent exception to iconicity worth noting. Predator alarm calls might seem a counterexample, since these bear no relation to any noises made by predators, or any other feature of predators. Accordingly, they share at least the arbitrariness of words, and may be important in an evolutionary sense: even if all they express is an emotional reaction to a predator, they may have been the first units to encode such information in a purely arbitrary way. To say this, however, is certainly not equivalent to claiming that alarm calls are a link between animal communication systems and language. It merely suggests that arbitrary symbolism had to begin somewhere, and that alarm calls are plausible candidates for first use.

As well as being iconic, many symbols of animal communication are gradient. That is to say, the length, pitch, or intensity of a call or communicative gesture will vary with the degree of emotion expressed. A bird determined to defend its territory to the death, for example, will sing louder and more continuously than one whose intent is weaker; the vigor with which bees dance will vary relative to the richness of the food source whose location they indicate.

The units of animal communication systems cannot (with one or two exceptions) be combined to yield additional meanings. A rare exception involves cotton-top tamarins; members of this monkey species can combine a chirp (used as an alarm call) with a squeak (used as a general alerting call) (Cleveland and Snowdon 1982). However, in contrast with the relative contextual and combinatorial freedom of the units of language, these calls can combine only after the alarm call has been given in isolation. The combination of alarm and alert therefore indicates no more than a state of continuing vigilance: it does not amount to a propositional statement. Moreover, the alerting call does not seem to combine with any other calls.[5] Yet there is no unit of language that will not (potentially at least) combine with a wide range of other units.

But most important, perhaps, the symbols of animal communication are discrete and bear no systematic relation to one another. Signs or calls seldom if ever consist of a merger or combination of two other signs or calls. There are no supersigns or supercalls expressing some general significance of which other signs or calls reflect particular types or aspects; for instance, there is no species (so far as we know) that has a generic call or sign for, say, "anger," and then a set of other calls or signs expressing anger at close kin, anger at a nonkin conspecific, anger at a member of another species, and so on.[6]

Although it is sometimes claimed that language incorporates a large iconic component, most linguists would agree that iconic representation constitutes a minor and peripheral part of language. The vast majority of linguistic symbols are arbitrary: they lack any apparent connection with the objects or actions they represent. There is no significant relationship between *perro, cachorro, chien,* and *hund,* and no way in which the sound or the form of any of these would suggest a small domestic animal; yet they mean "dog" in Spanish, Portuguese, French, and German respectively. (*Bow-wow* would of course be an example of an iconic symbol in this case, yet even onomatopoeic items vary from language to language— Anglophone roosters say *Cock-a-doodle-do* while Hispanophone ones say *Kokoriko.*) Human sign languages, which might be expected to exploit iconicity, seldom do so; even signs that begin as iconic tend to lose their iconicity quite quickly (Bellugi and Klima 1982).

Similarly, the symbols of language are not gradient. A *l-o-o-o-o-ng* jour- ney is not necessarily longer than a *long* journey (although the length- ening of the vowel might suggest to the hearer that the speaker *felt* the

5. It is worth noting that Snowdon (1993) dissociates himself from the con- tinuist interpretations that have sometimes been placed upon his work.

6. It may be that some species do show specific behaviors that indicate one or more of these particular types of anger, or that at least vary the intensity of expressions of anger in the different situations. However, one can predict with a fair amount of confidence that no animal communication system will be found to have a call or posture so abstract as to indicate anger in general. Indeed, the absurdity of supposing that such a system might contain such a unit (if it did, under what circumstances could it be used?) should help to highlight one of the many crucial differences between language and animal communication systems.

journey to be very long). I cannot indicate the relative corpulence of my acquaintances by saying that one is *fat*, another is *fa-at*, a third is *fa-a-at*, but a fourth is *fa-a-a-a-at*. Words like *warm* or *cool* are not intermediate in length, tone, or vowel quality as compared with the extremes of *hot* and *cold*.

Further, the symbols of language can be combined in a variety of ways. Sometimes the resultant combinations are the sum of the meanings of the items in isolation; thus a *wrongdoer* is simply a doer of wrongs. At other times they are not: a *sound bite* does not consist of the addition of a sound to a bite. (When words are combined to form sentences, the combinatorial possibilities are infinite, semantically as well as syntactically.)

Finally, the symbols of language do have subset-superset relations. Take a word like *insect*, for example, which belongs in the same set as *bird, fish, mammal*, and so on. *Insect* can be broken down into a list of more specific categories (*beetle, fly, wasp*, and so on) and these in turn into still more specific ones (*fly* into *tsetse* or *bluebottle, beetle* into *cockchafer, scarab*, or *bombardier*). The reason this last characteristic of language is so important has to do with the role of language as a representational system. By a representational system I mean an ordered picture of the world, arranged so that the items of information in it can be swiftly and easily located. A picture that divides our view of reality into named and readily recoverable pieces is what enables us to talk about the world and (more or less) everything in it—everything, at least, that lies within the reach of our senses, and even a good deal (angels, neutrinos, centaurs, and the like) that lies outside that reach.

But there is no sense in which we could call any other so-called language a representation of the world. Neither human body language nor the calls or gestures of monkeys represent the world. They represent how the human or monkey individual is feeling right now, and in so doing may transmit the wants or intentions of that individual, but no more than that. Only language can constitute a representation of the whole world that a creature senses and experiences.

Note that representation is logically prior to communication. We cannot communicate what we cannot first represent, because we would have no symbols with which to communicate it. This applies, not merely to human language, but to any of the so-called languages we have been discussing. Depilate an animal that expresses hostility by fluffing out its fur, and that animal cannot communicate hostility. Deprive us of our words (as some unfortunate individuals are deprived, by strokes or other traumas to the brain) and we cannot communicate linguistically. Let's imagine what would happen under some less drastic kind of intervention—say a pill which, if we swallowed it, would cause us to forget all words, but would otherwise leave our brains and bodies undamaged. Our senses would remain unimpaired; we would be able to see, hear, feel, taste, and touch everything as before. Our personalities would remain unaffected; we would have the same need and desire to communicate with our fellows—the birthright of all social species. Our vocal organs would remain in tip-top condition; we would be able to make a range of sounds identical to those we made before.

But none of this would profit us in the slightest. We would put our vocal organs to work, familiar sounds would come out, but none of them would mean anything. We would stare in wonder at the babbling of others just as they would at ours.

Words, thoughts, and images

One might say, "Well, this proves my point. We would still have things to communicate, but we would simply have lost the means by which to communicate them." It is very natural (and has seemed so at least since Plato, perhaps the first who recorded this view of things),[7] to feel you have a whole flock of thoughts floating around in your head and all you have to do is catch the one you want, dress it out in words, and send it (vocally or orthographically) into the world. It is also natural to feel that the sun goes around the earth (though we have trained ourselves to disbelieve that) or that humans are too special to be descended from apes (some of us still have not trained ourselves to disbelieve that). And for this belief in preverbal thought there is indeed more justification than for many other popular beliefs. Thinking can go on in the absence of language, otherwise no nonhuman (and, for that matter, no infant

7. I am thinking in particular of Plato's metaphor of the aviary in *Theaetetus*. Of course, on another reading, one might claim that Plato's "birds"—the ideas that float around in our minds, and that will not always come when called for—are in fact already in the form of linguistic representations, in which case there would be no disagreement with the position taken here. But many writers, even among the most linguistically sophisticated (e.g., Fodor 1975, Jackendoff 1987, Pinker 1989), have seen thought as existing independently of language (even though they have used the term "language of thought"). The issues raised here are important and will be dealt with more thoroughly in subsequent chapters.

human) could think; and to claim that they cannot think would be absurd.

The way the question is often put could hardly have been better designed if it had been deliberately intended to confuse the issue: "Is there thought without language?" The real questions, which this book will try to answer, are: Is *all* thinking the same? Is there a qualitative difference between the thinking of animals and humans? And if there is, could that difference have anything to do with the fact that animals don't have language, while humans do?

Many people claim things like, "I don't think in words, I think in images. Of course I can translate that into words, after the fact, if I want to, but what does that prove?" Let's say you are one of those who think they think in images. You have an image of a cat on a mat, and indeed you can immediately dress it out as "The cat sat on the mat." If words failed you, you could draw it; if drawing failed, you might be able to point to actual cats and mats in the room.

But such a test is too easy. Take something more like "My trust in you has been shattered forever by your unfaithfulness." Now have the mental image to which this sentence corresponds. My guess is that either your mind went blank or you merely ran through the sentence again, or one very like it. But that would be thinking in words, and you just said you don't do that. Maybe you thought in exactly the same terms on both occasions, and the "image" in the first case was merely an epiphenomenal consequence of the imageability of cats and mats.

But what about the feeling that the second sentence described? Could you even have had that feeling, that precise feeling—not just a vague sense of resentment but the uniquely hurtful sense of betrayal that an act of infidelity provokes—if you did not know what trust was, or what unfaithfulness was, or what it meant for trust to be shattered? While there may be some thoughts and feelings we can have without language, there are infinitely many that we cannot. If it comes to that, even "The cat sat on the mat" turns out to be not such a clear case as it might have seemed.

Philosopher Daniel Dennett (1991:27) developed a neat trick to illustrate the pitfalls that attach to thinking in images. (The purposes for which he uses it are slightly different from mine, but that doesn't matter.) Imagine, he says, a purple cow, in as much detail as you can. Now say which way the cow was facing, whether it was chewing cud, whether its udder was visible, and what exact shade of purple it was. Many people do the imagining so lazily, Dennett says, that they can't answer these questions. So this time do a good job on the cat on the mat. Was it Persian, Siamese, or common-or-garden tabby? Were its whiskers long or short? Did it have a satisfied or dissatisfied expression? Did it look well fed? Was the mat a doormat? What color was it? Did it have a pattern on it, and if so, what was the pattern?

Now translate your thought into words. It cannot be translated simply as "The cat sat on the mat." Is *that* cat Persian, Siamese, or tabby? Is the mat a doormat, a floormat, or a carmat? No, you say, it's "just a cat" and "just a mat." But there is nothing in nature that is just a cat or just a mat. Everything that is a cat has to be some kind of cat, Siamese or Persian or whatever, and it has to have all of its own (temporary or permanent) individual features. The same goes for every mat. But the more specific your image, the less it is like what you intended to say. If you wanted to think the thing you were going to say, you would have had to imagine vague blobs with the labels "cat" and "mat" on them. Or, as Dennett suggests, you would think something like "I'm imagining a purple cow" (or cat). But THAT'S THINKING IN WORDS! So you merely thought you were thinking a thought and dressing it up in language.

And that's not all. The sentence said "The cat sat on the mat." That means that the cat is no longer sitting on the mat. How exactly did your image convey *this* piece of information? Did the cat sit there a while and then get up and walk away? (This would correspond to "The cat was sitting on the mat but then got up and walked away.") Or, more likely, the issue of time did not occur to you. Now that it has, how would your image distinguish "The cat sat on the mat" from "The cat is sitting on the mat" or "The cat will sit on the mat"? For that matter, how would it distinguish "The cat is sitting on the mat" from "The mat is lying underneath the cat"? The images are surely identical, but the sentences are not.

So, even in the seemingly simple cases, it is not true that we build up a picture of the world and then dress it out in language. Rather, language builds us the picture of the world that we use for thinking and communicating; we can then, if we please, fancy that we see this picture also (or instead) in terms of images. And in any case, Dennett's point was precisely this: you only fancy those images, and even the idea that you can have images in your head (whether to "think in" or otherwise) is misguided. There's no color in there, no light to see by, no eyes to see with. For that matter, there are no words in there either—we'll see in

Chapter 3 that there is a big difference between thinking in language and thinking with words. All you have in there are trains of electrochemical impulses; they may *represent* other things, but they do not *constitute* those things, yet they are all you have to think with.

There are, presumably, ensembles of neurons whose firing represents concepts. Recent work (e.g., Ojeman and Creutzfeld 1987, Damasio 1990, Hart and Gordon 1992) suggests that several such ensembles representing the same concept may be scattered through the brain: there may, for instance, be an auditory cat and a visual cat as well as a linguistic cat. Note that the linguistic cat is a different kettle of fish from the other mental cats. The linguistic cat is also a holistic cat. Ask me about the word *cat* and I can tap my auditory knowledge ("It purrs, it miaows"), my visual knowledge ("It's usually black, brown, or gray—seldom if ever puce or scarlet"), and so forth. The word ties together aspects of catness that may well be stored separately in other areas of the brain, suggesting that its neural representation may serve as what has been called a *convergence zone* (Damasio and Damasio 1992).

Is there a holistic nonlinguistic cat as well as a holistic linguistic cat? If we could answer this question, we could shed a good deal of light on what goes on in human thinking. Until we can find the answer, there are at least a few reasons (some of which will be touched on in subsequent chapters) for thinking that the only holistic cat is the linguistic cat—or in other words, that it takes some kind of arbitrary symbol to tie together all the representations of all the attributes that make up our idea of "cat." And we do know for sure that in the case of trust or unfaithfulness, there can be nothing beneath the linguistic concept except other linguistic representations, because abstract nouns have no perceptual attributes to be attached to them and therefore no possible representation outside those areas of the brain devoted to language.

Notice there are several things that I do *not* mean by "linguistic concept." I do not mean the mode of storage of the phonological word /k/-/ae/-/t/; this is just another ensemble of neurons that is triggered when I want to say "cat" rather than just think it, and that if fired fires other neurons in the part of the motor system that controls vocalization. The separateness of such representations from semantic representations is shown in the ways people distinguish words from nonwords (Forster 1976) and by the fact that slips of the tongue fall into two distinct classes, one phonological (substituting *sympathy* for *symphony* or *bodies* for *bot-*

tles) and one semantic (*read* for *written* or *fringe* for *verge*) (Garrett 1978). Nor do I mean a kind of warehouse of predicates that would exhaustively describe "cat": "is a member of the feline family," "likes milk," "hunts mice," "is roughly the size of a football," "has fur," "purrs," "scratches you when irritated," and so on.

I mean a set of neurons in the language area preferentially linked to other sets, some near and some far, some also in the language area and some in other areas, so that at the prompt "cat" (on a screen, or through a pair of headphones) or by merely happening to think of a cat, I can access all the predicates listed in the previous paragraph. That this level of representation is quite separate and differently organized from sensory representations is shown not only by patients with lesions (Hart and Gordon 1992) but also by the study of semantic priming in normals (Wernick and Daniel 1970, Morton and Patterson 1980). Although words will be more quickly identified when preceded by a word of related meaning ("nurse" will be recognized more quickly if preceded by "doctor" than if preceded by "table"), visual presentation of objects will not speed recognition even when word and image have the same referent: recognition of a picture of a butterfly immediately prior to presentation of the word "butterfly" does not reduce the number of milliseconds it takes to recognize that word. Exactly *how* linguistic concepts are represented remains unclear, alas.

That I can access such predicates ("likes milk," "purrs," and so forth) when prompted by "cat" is one of those facts that are taken for granted, and only noticed when as a result of some trauma or dementia the access fails. And yet it is an extremely marvelous fact that I do not have to cast about in my mind ("Hm . . . has webbed feet? . . . lives in the Arctic? . . . is about the size of a taxi? . . .") in order to describe and list all the attributes of "cat." It is all done for me, as if by magic. But it is not magic. We have wiring diagrams that look more like Figure 1.1b than Figure 1.1a (1a represents, as far as one can extricate it from its remarkably inexplicit descriptions, the kind of from-thought-to-word process that seems quite widely accepted, and tries to give it an explicit wiring-diagram interpretation).

Figure 1.1b, or something similar, would seem to represent the kind of infrastructure needed to support our picture of the world. It should now be clear why the symbolic units from which that picture is built have to

Figure 1.1

Relations between thought and word

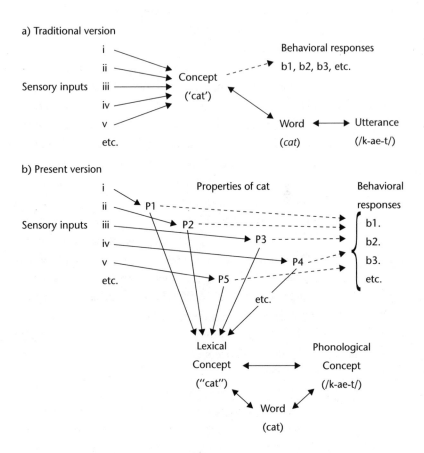

a) Traditional version

b) Present version

be noniconic, nongradient, interrelated, and orders of magnitude more numerous than the symbolic units used in systems of animal communication. Those units have to be numerous because there is so much in the world to represent. If they are so numerous, they are more economically produced by recombining a small number of fairly abstract units (in vocal language, speech sounds; in sign language, hand shapes) than by assigning unrelated representations to each unit. This rules out iconicity as a major strategy. If they are to reduce the complexity of the sensory world to a manageable level of simplicity, they must categorize. This rules out gradient, nondiscrete units. If units are to be readily recoverable they must be filed hierarchically, not thrown together like junk in a closet. This enforces the kind of interrelatedness of levels noted in previous discussion of *insect-fly-bluebottle* and the like.

But wait! There's more! You get syntax too!

Everything described so far lies, partly if by no means completely, within the potential range of other species. Creatures as diverse as chimpanzees (Premack 1972), bonobos (Greenfield and Savage-Rumbaugh 1990), gorillas (Patterson and Linden 1981), orangutans (Miles 1983), sea lions (Schusterman and Krieger 1984), dolphins (Herman et al. 1984), and African grey parrots (Pepperberg 1987) have shown themselves able, with adequate training, to acquire symbolic systems that include at least some of the properties mentioned above as properties of human language. Units used in such systems have been noniconic, nongradient, and, if less numerous than the units of language, at least considerably more numerous than the symbols of any recorded animal communication system. Moreover, those units have sometimes carried factual information (rather than merely information about the animal's current state), although one has to admit that what apes choose to communicate voluntarily is almost always about something they want to do or eat. On occasion the units have even shown signs of subset-superset relations (Savage-Rumbaugh 1986, reporting her experiments with apes Sherman and Austin).

The apparatus so far described does not merely provide symbolic representations for categories of objects and actions. That apparatus, perhaps with an assist from some other quarter, also enables us to string symbols together to form simple propositions. Exactly what additional mechanisms, if any, are required for this makes a topic of some interest but little clarity, at least for the present.[8] It is a remarkable but wholly unexplained fact that of the fairly wide range of creatures mentioned in the previous paragraph, all seem to have been able, once they

8. Edelman (1989:147–48) discusses what he calls "presyntax," but he is quite unexplicit about the properties he attributes to this. Since he seems to believe, following Lieberman (1984, 1991), that nothing beyond the addition of an anatomically modern vocal tract was required to turn presyntax into syntax, it is far from clear that his presyntax is in any way comparable to the stringing together of symbols that I have in mind here.

had acquired symbolic units, to form simple propositions without further explicit instruction. So far as one can tell from the literature, animals were simply exposed to the multisign utterances of their trainers.

No purpose would be served here by speculating about this mysterious latency of propositional structure. The point I want to make is that while such structure makes possible a few simple propositions, it is wholly inadequate to support propositions of any complexity; hence its usefulness is limited, whether for communication or for thinking.

The reasons for this deserve some consideration. What "language"-trained animals seem to do is attach symbols to one another consecutively, as one might add beads to a string. In some cases one can discern what looks like a topic-comment structure: the utterer may begin with a symbol referring to some relatively familiar entity or one that forms the current focus of attention, then add another symbol with a less familiar or less predictable referent. Often one encounters patterns that do seem to have been directly modeled by trainers, such as an apparent regularity in the ordering of thematic roles, along the lines of actor-action-recipient of action, or actor-action-location.

If an animal frequently and regularly produces sequences such as *me eat orange*, while only occasionally and randomly producing sequences such as *me orange eat*, *orange me eat*, or *eat orange me*, it might indeed seem tempting to suggest that such an animal had internalized the order actor-action-recipient or had even mastered basic syntax, since actor-action-recipient might be regarded, in grammatical terms, as subject-verb-object. Such suggestions are still made (Fouts 1983, Greenfield and Savage-Rumbaugh 1990), if less frequently than they were in the early 1970s, largely as a consequence of Terrace et al. (1979), wherein it was concluded that apes cannot produce sentences. A more modest claim would be that creatures with such capacities have acquired what in Bickerton (1990) I called *protolanguage*, a medium for expressing propositions that remains distinct from, and inferior to, full human language (I avoid here the common term *natural language*, as protolanguage is no less natural than full language).

For when we compare examples of protolanguage with examples of full human language (henceforth simply "language"), we can observe a number of features, frequent if not universal in language, that the propositions of trained animals (or for that matter, the propositions of adult pidgin speakers[9] and human infants, which represent other varieties of protolanguage) lack entirely. First and most obvious is length of utterance: while language utterances are potentially infinite in length, protolanguage utterances are restricted to a few syllables.

Nor is this restriction a fortuitous one. Any unit of language can be expanded indefinitely: from *dogs* we can proceed to *big dogs*, thence to *very big dogs*, thence to *very big brown dogs*, thence to *very big brown dogs with long hair*, thence to *very big brown dogs with long hair that bark loudly*, and so on, indefinitely. Similarly, a sentence like *Mary knows Bill* can be expanded into *John thinks that Mary knows Bill*, and *Sue believes that John thinks that Mary knows Bill*, and *Joe admits that Sue believes that John thinks that Mary knows Bill*, and *I wonder whether Joe admits . . .* , and so on. The only limit on our ability to continue these embeddings of one phrase or sentence within another lies, not in our mechanisms for expanding phrases or sentences (which simply involve infinite recursion), but rather in our ability to process and interpret the products of those mechanisms.

Then there is fluency. Characteristically (exceptions may arise for reasons that have nothing to do with language per se), language is highly fluent, deliverable at median rates of a hundred words per minute or more, with negligible hesitation and self-correction. Protolanguage utterances, on the other hand, are always disfluent, with frequent pauses, hesitations, and reformulations. This is understandable only if there are mechanisms for generating fluent speech that are absent or somehow rendered inoperative in protolanguage.

A third difference lies in interpretability. Language is almost always interpretable by a native speaker of the relevant variety (or even a fluent nonnative speaker), even in the complete absence of contextual information. The same is by no means true of protolanguage, despite its lesser complexity. The difference in interpretability arises from a combination of factors.

9. The definition of a pidgin language is generally given as "a makeshift, structurally impoverished contact language which is not the native language of any of its speakers." See note 12 for further references. I have argued elsewhere (Bickerton 1981, 1984, 1990) that at least in its early stages, which are the relevant ones for present purposes, pidgin structure is not just impoverished but nonexistent, and the pidgin itself is not a true human language in the sense of the present discussion.

In language, propositions consist of a verb and one or more arguments of that verb (argument, in this context, means any expression that refers to any participant in an action, state, or event, whether that participant performs an action, undergoes it, is its goal or beneficiary, is the instrument with which it is performed, or plays any other role in such an action, state, or event). While some argument roles are optional (typically, though not always, time, location, instrument, beneficiary, and so on), others may be obligatory in the case of particular verbs (such as Agent, "who or what performs an action with an object"; Patient or Theme, "who or what undergoes or experiences the action"; and Goal, "who or what is the end point, or receives the result of the action"). For instance, intransitive verbs such as *walk* or *sleep* take a single obligatory argument, transitive verbs such as *write* or *break* take two, and ditransitive verbs (verbs that take both direct and indirect objects) like *give* or *put* take three.

In language, either all the obligatory arguments of a given verb are expressed or, if one is omitted, the missing argument is recoverable by rule. For instance, in *I want to see Mary*, no Agent for *see* is expressed, but we know that the verb *see* must have an Agent and it must be an Agent that is coreferential with the subject of the main verb *want*. Similarly, in *What do you want to do?*, no Theme argument follows *do* immediately, in the position reserved for Theme arguments, but again we know that *do* requires a Theme argument and it must be identical with *what* (indeed, we may sometimes even say *You want to do what?*). The process involved forms part of what is known as semantic interpretation, another of those linguistic processes that we use hundreds of times a day and take completely for granted without ever pausing to consider how marvelous they really are.

Notice that I did *not* say "linguistic processes that we use them hundreds of times a day and take them completely for granted without ever pausing to consider how marvelous they really are." Nor did I say "linguistic processes that we use hundreds of times a day and take completely for granted without ever pausing to consider how marvelous really are." We look at those two examples and know it is wrong to include the first two third-person pronouns in the first example, and equally wrong to leave out "they" in the second. There are eight possible distributions of pronouns and gaps for that sentence, and only one of them is right. How do we know that? Is this some ridiculous rule of prescriptive grammar that we learned in school? Certainly not. You never saw my original sentence or maybe even one remotely like it before, yet you know that the two variations (plus five other incorrect ones not included here) are just not English sentences.

Determining which of the eight possibilities is the only right one is a feat we could perform only by virtue of having some internal mechanism that told us, quite automatically, where the pronouns were right and where they were wrong. This marvelous process works so well that we never notice the difference between the times when we are obliged to refer to things overtly and those when we may (and often must) leave them unexpressed—"understood" as they used to say in the grammar books of old.[10]

But in protolanguage, this mechanism is inoperative. Arguments of verbs may be inserted or omitted at will. When an argument is omitted, no regular process enables us to recover it. For example, the verb *hit* requires (at least) two arguments, Agent and Theme, a hitter and a hittee. A common type of protolanguage utterance, such as *man hit*, clearly lacks one or the other of these. But which? Since protolanguage utterances have no principled order (although they may have a statistically preponderant order, which of course is not the same thing), we have no way of determining whether the intended utterance was *(A) man hit (someone)* or *(Someone) hit (a) man*. Only prior knowledge of the situation described enables us to interpret the utterance correctly.

Finally, the nature of the constituent units distinguishes between language and protolanguage. In protolanguage, almost all (usually, all) units carry specific reference to categories of object or occurrence supposedly occurring in the real world. None of the units make reference to the structure of utterances, for there is no structure to which reference can be made. In language, roughly half of all units (on a token, not a type, basis) refer to the structure of utterances and contain negligible if any reference to external-world categories.[11]

10. For a discussion of these "understood" items, or "empty categories," as they are more commonly known, see Chomsky (1981, 1986); a more user-friendly source is Radford (1988).

11. On a type basis, grammatical items amount to at most a few hundred, as compared to the many thousands of lexical items in any language. It follows that the list of the ten most frequently used units in any language would consist of grammatical rather than lexical items.

Thus coordinating conjunctions such as *but, and,* or *or* indicate that a structural unit similar and equal to the last structural unit is about to appear. (They may, additionally, show whether an additive or alternative relationship holds between the conjuncts.) Subordinating conjunctions such as *that, unless,* or *because* show that another clause, either a required complement (*Bill said [that he was hungry]*) or an optional adjunct (*Bill left [because he was hungry]*) is about to appear. Prepositions like *of* in *reversal of fortune* or *to* in *martyr to indigestion* do not entail possession or direction of movement, as they might seem to do in *a pencil of mine* or *to the train station*; they merely indicate a close relationship between two nouns, usually showing that they form part of a single argument with a head-modifier structure (the head preceding *of,* the modifier following) rather than constituting two separate arguments (as in *It's enough to give even a martyr indigestion*). The only sense in which we can say that words like *that* or *of* "mean" anything is the sense in which we say things like "That cloud means rain"—a sense very different from that of usages such as "*Weimaraner* means a particular type of dog."

Of course, when most nonlinguists (and even, I'm ashamed to say, some linguists) talk about syntax, matters like these are not usually uppermost in the discussion. What nonlinguists usually understand by syntax is mere regularity of word order. But regularity of word order is the most trivial thing about syntax. Indeed you could argue that it does not form part of syntax at all, since there are human languages (so-called nonconfigurational or scrambling languages) that allow almost completely free word order yet clearly possess all the diagnostic features of syntax listed above. The fact that most languages tend to have a fairly consistent word order arises, I suspect, more from general principles of harmony and symmetry than from any syntactic mechanism. Even those languages that are "strict configurational," like English, allow for considerable variation in order: we can say YOU BAKED a CAKE for ME or YOU BAKED ME a CAKE or For ME YOU BAKED a CAKE or A CAKE was what YOU BAKED for ME or BAKED a CAKE for ME was what YOU did or A CAKE was BAKED for ME by YOU or BAKED ME a CAKE YOU sure did—seven out of the twenty-four theoretically possible orderings of *you, bake, me,* and *cake,* yet all seven share the same meaning.

The characteristics reviewed above, rather than mere regularity of ordering, are what make the sharp distinction that I have claimed exists between language and protolanguage—a distinction which (not coincidentally, one assumes) also marks the boundary between humans and nonhumans. That boundary may at first seem to be blurred by the existence of some humans (children under two, pidgin speakers, some of the mentally retarded) who are capable only of protolanguage. However, each of these apparent exceptions has a simple and straightforward explanation.

If the mechanism that generates mature syntax does not come on line until around age two, the protolanguage productions of pre-twos are predicted. If the mechanism that generates mature syntax requires a detailed lexicon for its expression, the protolanguage productions of pidgin speakers are similarly predicted, since pidgins arise when speakers have only a very limited access to some common lexicon (pidgin speakers are invariably also fluent speakers of one or more full human languages).[12] Finally, and most significant, if language is what underlies characteristically human thought and consciousness (as subsequent chapters will argue), we would expect to find that certain types of mental retardation or brain damage are accompanied by striking deficits in language, and particularly in syntax.

However, the distinguishing characteristics we have discussed are only superficial features, symptomatic of the mechanisms that underlie language in humans and the absence of such mechanisms in other species. To merely note such features is far from determining whence they arise or what those underlying mechanisms consist of. But as we seek to determine the nature of those mechanisms, we are faced with conceptual problems of a rather common type.

So what is syntax and where does it come from?

Writers in the behavioral sciences continue to speak of humans creating or inventing language, implying that the processes are much the same as those involved in creating or inventing works of art or novel technologies. Countless arguments have been elaborated (by Chomsky 1965, 1975, 1986, etc.; Lenneberg 1967; Lightfoot 1982; Pinker 1993; Smith and Wilson 1979, among others) to demonstrate that language

---

12. For a discussion of pidginization and associated phenomena from the present perspective, see Bickerton (1983a, 1984, 1988). Rather different views are presented by some other writers (Hall 1966, Whinnom 1971, Romaine 1988, Muhlhausler 1986, etc.).

could have come into existence only as a species-specific, biologically based phenomenon, emerging as automatically as upright walking or the ability to grasp and manipulate objects. I do not propose to add anything here, except a small examination which scholars of human behavior should be required to pass before they are allowed to write about the creation or invention of language. It goes as follows:

Question One: Explain how, and why, the inventors of language arranged things so that *John wants someone to work for* means "John wants someone such that he, John, can work for that person" while *John wants someone to work for him* means "John wants someone such that that person will work for him, John." State how you yourself learned the reversal of meaning in the subordinate clause and show how its invention was culturally and/or biologically adaptive.

Question Two: Discuss the two sentences *Which letters did Bill destroy without reading?* and *Which letters did Bill destroy without reading them?* Given that the inventors of language made the two sentences in Question One mean two different things, describe the benefits those inventors gained by making the two sentences in this question mean the same.

Question Three: If the inventors of language made it possible for you to say *Mary is someone that people like as soon as they see* and *Mary is someone that people like as soon as they see her*, why didn't they also make it possible to say *Mary is someone that people like her as soon as they see*? Explain in detail how the far-reaching cultural, social, and economic advantages obtained by allowing the first pair of sentences would have been frustrated if the latter sentence had been permitted.[13]

The point I am trying to make is that when people who have not been exposed to modern linguistics write about language, they write

13. Readers who wish to defend the "clever invention" hypothesis should not fall into the trap of dismissing these examples as mere bizarre oddities of English that can be safely ignored as having no consequence for the great "communicative" functions of language. They are not, and cannot be. They merely represent specific instantiations, in English, of universal principles affecting what are known as "empty categories" (the "understood" constituents of traditional grammars)— principles discussed at length in the works of Chomsky cited above. If it were not for such abstract principles, our communicative efforts would be clogged by masses of redundant proper names and pronouns. But since it has taken some of our best minds many years to come near figuring out what those principles are, the possibility that still smarter humans invented them countless thousands of years ago can be dismissed with the contempt it deserves.

as if on some mountaintop from which language, spread out on the plains below, is but a misty blur, deprived of the knotty peculiarities with which we linguists have to wrestle in our daily toil. All that they see is the Big Picture: "[O]ur physical and social environment [has] become so complex that a really complex language is required to deal with it" (Wills 1993:294). Well, nobody doubts that society is complex and language is complex, but do these two complexities have anything to do with one another? Are society and language complex in the same ways? Does the kind of complexity we find in language, when we come down off the mountaintop and survey it up close—the kind illustrated in my examination questions above—help us unravel the complexities we encounter in our daily lives? What kind of person or persons would have or could have invented just those kinds of linguistic complexity, and who would have followed them if they had? Until questions such as these can receive sensible answers, remarks like the one by Wills are empty rhetoric.

Besides, if there were any link between cultural complexity and linguistic complexity, we would expect to find that the most complex societies had the most complex languages while simpler societies had simpler languages. We do not find any such thing. In the first place, nobody has managed to produce a metric for linguistic simplicity. If you measure this by one feature you are refuted by another. If you measure by the number and variety of inflections, then English and Chinese, the languages of two highly complex cultures, are extremely simple; if you look at their syntax, it's another story. Simplicity over here always seems to be paid for by complexity over there. When you take all aspects into account, languages are roughly equal in complexity. In the second place, closely related languages that are almost identical in structure are often found in the most complex societies and the simplest. Edward Sapir (1921) put this most forcefully by noting that when it comes to language, "Plato walks with the Macedonian swineherd, and Lao-Tze with the head-hunter of Assam."

Anyone who looks at language up close must conclude that the complexities of language are its own special complexities, arising from sources very different from the desire, conscious or otherwise, to make complex cultures manipulable. And the most plausible explanation for those special complexities is that they are conditions imposed by the mechanism that produces them—by the workings of the organ that is the sole begetter of sentences, the human brain. In other words, language is the way it is because that is the only way the brain can do it.

And that way is not necessarily the optimal way. If language is the way it is because the brain just does it that way, we should not expect the results to be optimal for communication or anything else. The way our brain, or anything else's brain, does things is the way it is because that's the way the brain evolved. You might argue that the brain is a purpose-built machine: if it hadn't done anything that served the purposes of its original owners, it would not have evolved in the first place. True, but when new purposes came along, there was no technological wizard to devise a wholly novel Mark 2 brain. The human brain is wall-to-wall add-ons, a maze of dinguses and gizmos patched into the original pattern of a primitive fish brain. No wonder it isn't easy to understand how it works.

As an example of what I mean we might consider the so-called garden path sentences (Bever and Langendoen 1971), for example, *The horse raced past the barn fell*. The first time you hear or read the sentence, you think it is ungrammatical, or nonsense. You may not realize the truth until someone points out that this sentence is structurally analogous to *The planet discovered by the astronomer disappeared*. The difficulty arises because while *the planet discovered by the astronomer* is clearly not a sentence, *the horse raced past the barn* could be. That's how you parsed all but the last word of the sentence, and then when *fell* got unexpectedly added, you didn't know what to do with it and your parsing mechanism went haywire.

Another way to demystify the sentence is to expand it: *The horse THAT WAS raced past the barn fell*. In other words, the subject of *fell* is the whole rest of the sentence: the head noun *horse* and the relative clause attached to it. Normally in English it is okay to leave out a relative pronoun or the *that* that marks relative clauses. We can say *the guy who/that I saw yesterday*, but probably we will just say *the guy I saw yesterday*. It's a different story if *guy* is the subject of the relative clause. We say *The guy I saw yesterday was Bill's brother* but we don't say *The guy saw me yesterday was Bill's brother*. That is another garden path sentence, not as hard to process as the horse-and-barn example, but still something that any serious creator of language would program out of the system.

If language were optimally planned for communication you would think that every language, like English, would have an obligatory marker like a relative pronoun that would tell folk, "Hey, look out! What's coming isn't the rest of the main clause, it's only a relative clause!" But in fact there are languages that have no such marker; for that matter, as Bever and Langendoen point out, there was a time, a few hundred years ago, when even English allowed such sentences without any kind of relative clause marker. People have a hard time with unmarked relative clauses; language does not. Indeed, it may even prefer them.

Elsewhere I have argued that creole languages—new languages that arise when children receive a chaotic and virtually structureless pidgin as part of their linguistic input—stand closer to the archetypal pattern of human language than older and more established languages do (Bickerton 1984, 1988). In their earliest stages, creoles simply do not mark relative clauses, regardless of whether the head noun is the subject or the object of the clause. For instance, one speaker of Hawaii Creole English that I know produced the sentence *The guy gon' lay the vinyl been quote me price*. Not *The guy WHO gon' lay the vinyl*—to him, that would have been ungrammatical. It's true that creoles usually make up new relative-clause markers, but they take their time doing it—sometimes a couple of hundred years or more. On the other hand, creoles make up markers of tense immediately.

The most natural conclusion to draw from this is that language can do without relative-clause markers but it does need things like tense. Language can make relative clauses just fine with the aid of what is called a null operator (Chomsky 1986), a kind of relative pronoun that is about as accessible to the senses as the average neutrino. Overt relative-clause markers are just things that people generally tack on to their languages, sooner or later, and that become obligatory in certain contexts, precisely because they are useful for communication. Language tolerates them, but they are, if you like, purpose-built: natural enough, but certainly no more natural than their absence—perhaps even less so.

Why language should need tense markers but not relative-clause markers is something that is quite impossible to explain in terms of social, cultural, or communicative benefits. Anyone purpose-building a language could make a much better case for a converse state of affairs: relative-clause markers would be obligatory but tense markers could be freely omitted unless time was not obvious from the context or needed to be specified for discourse reasons. Philosopher Willard Quine, for one, could never understand why every sentence should have to be marked with tense of some kind (Quine 1960:170). But for some mysterious reason that doubtless lies hidden in the history of brain evolution, language simply reverses the communicative priorities.

We can reasonably conclude, then, that syntax, the very core of human language—that which distinguishes language most clearly from attempts by animals to produce language—cannot be a mere clever invention produced by smart humans as a consequence of their having big brains (a belief still widely held in the behavioral sciences). If it is not an invention, it must be something the brain does automatically. If the brain does it automatically, then the brain must have evolved in certain specific ways that make possible the automatic production of language. If the brains of countless succeeding generations produce language in accord with the same invariant structural principles (no matter how much the superficial details of sounds and vocabulary may change), we can assume that the brain mechanisms that determine language are genetically transmitted.

The existence of so-called feral children who are incapable of speech (Malson 1972) is no argument against this. Countless biological processes depend on some form of environmental triggering. In the case of language, such triggering can be quite minimal. Deaf children of hearing parents, unexposed to any form of sign language, have created primitive forms of such languages even when their linguistic input was zero (Goldin-Meadow 1979); deaf children exposed to primitive sign systems have developed these into full-fledged natural languages (Kegl and Iwata 1989). Children in many countries exposed to primitive, early-stage pidgins have converted these into full natural languages (Bickerton 1981, 1984). Hearing children exposed to a macaronic jargon in Hawaii (Roberts 1995) developed a creole language in a single generation (Roberts 1993).

A word about the last case is perhaps in order. While forms of sign language are still being created today, the particular social circumstances that trigger the emergence of a creole language (a multilingual community with no common language and without an accessible target language) have not occurred for several decades and seem unlikely to occur in the near future. Accordingly, the birth of creole languages has to be reconstructed, and is therefore a controversial subject (for views opposed to that of this author, see Lefebvre 1986, Holm 1988, Singler 1992). However, recent archival research by Julian Roberts (1993, 1995) has unearthed many hundreds of verbatim citations of contemporary speech by residents of all ethnic groups in Hawaii during the period (1880-1920) immediately before, during, and after the emergence of Hawaii Creole English (HCE). It is clear that a structureless macaronic jargon prevailed among most adults in Hawaii throughout that period, that no adult speech anticipated the characteristic forms and structures of HCE, and that those forms and structures all emerged in the speech of the generation born in the early 1890s.

A telling example is the case of a Portuguese father who, in 1897 on the island of Kauai, discovered his small son in possession of a nickel (a suspiciously large sum at a time when workers earned a dollar a day). Questioned about how he got it, the boy said "One kanaka make me one bad thing inside of house" (the statement is preserved in the transcript of the consequent sex-abuse trial in the records of the Fourth Circuit Court of Hawaii). This use of *one* as an indefinite article is found in practically every creole language throughout the world, but not in *any* of the hundreds of Hawaii citations prior to 1897, which contain no indefinite articles of any kind; and even for some time after that date it is found only in the speech of young persons. In other words, a child, without any model, created a type of phrase, indefinite-article-plus-noun, in the same way (using the number *one* as an indefinite article) as other children did, quite independently, in several other communities widely scattered around the globe.

When data of this kind are added to all the other considerations detailed above, the conclusion is surely inescapable that syntax constitutes a biologically based attribute of the species in just the sense that upright posture and an opposable thumb do—no more, no less.

Language and communication revisited

It should be appropriately deflating to human self-importance to discover that what crucially distinguishes us from other species is not something lofty and philosophical like "meaning," but something quite mechanical: the unconscious, mindless cranking out of formal syntactic patterns.

But it is this mechanism that underlies all distinctively human behavior. "Only connect," said E. M. Forster in the epigraph to *Howards End*. Syntax only connects, but without its connections there would be very little for us to communicate. With it, we are able to talk about anything under the sun without attending to the means whereby we put our sentences together. And the persons listening to us can understand everything we say without any assistance from linguistic or extralinguistic context or pragmatic knowledge or anything else—in stark contrast to the utterances of pidgin speakers, children under two, or trained apes, which may need massive doses of context to interpret. True language can be interpreted directly because syntax provides us with a host of structural clues that always suffice to tell us who did what, and with which, and to whom—clues that are provided automatically, indeed obligatorily, by the abstract structures that the syntactic mechanism produces.

It should be clear from the foregoing that the belief, so widely held and frequently repeated, that "language is (a means of) communication" is wrong in a way that has been devastating to any adequate conception of what humans are and how they differ from other species. Communication is just one use to which language can be put (and distinguishing between a thing and its uses should surely form the most basic step in any analysis). There are many other uses, of course: two that will receive special attention in later chapters are the enhancement of intelligence and the creation of our peculiar form of consciousness. Indeed, what this book proposes to do is simply to stand the conventional wisdom of the behavioral sciences on its head: instead of the human species growing clever enough to invent language, it will view that species as blundering into language and, as a direct result of that, becoming clever. But since intelligence and consciousness form part of human cognition, and since, as Donald (1991:1) rightly points out, "We cannot understand . . . cognitive capacities without accounting for their place in the biological order," discussion of such things must be postponed until we have considered how the language that makes them possible might have evolved.

Chapter 2

Language and evolution

In the Introduction I suggested that the behavioral sciences have failed to give an adequate account of human nature at least partly because of the conjunction and mutual reinforcement of two widespread beliefs: that language is simply a means of communication and that human intelligence is the result of the rapid growth and unusual size of human brains. Hopefully, the previous chapter undermined the first belief. A review of some well-known evolutionary facts should perform a similar service for the second.

Indeed, doubts about the first belief should have removed some support from the second. For the second belief depends largely on the following line of reasoning: if our enormous brains are the source of our intelligence, and if that intelligence is powerful enough to account for the extraordinary development of our species, it is absurd to suppose that language, a mere means of communication, could have given rise to it; human intelligence must therefore be attributed to other faculties residing within those enormous brains. What could such faculties be? The behavioral sciences go off on a wild-goose chase after mysterious "reasoning powers," "inference engines," "cognitive faculties"—things that may have no independent existence and may have arisen as epiphenomena of language.

The brain-growth fallacy

The best way to deal with the brain-size/intelligence equation is by looking at human evolution. Around three and a half million years ago our ancestors were already walking upright, but their brains were little larger than the brains of contemporary apes. Over the course of the last three million years or so, those brains more than tripled in size, yielding the highest brain-body ratio of any species on earth.

Why this fast growth? One might as well ask why giraffes developed long necks, or why peacocks developed long tails. They just did, that's all. Genetic accidents happen, and if a change results that confers an advantage, such a change can persist. Indeed, it may persist even if it doesn't confer an advantage—even, in some cases, if it causes a disadvantage. The peacock's tail, for example, severely inhibits the mobility of peacocks, but is favored, apparently, because peahens liked bigger and gaudier tails, assuming that any male that could put up with such a handicap and still function efficiently must constitute good breeding stock (Cronin 1992).

Indeed Ridley (1993) explicitly claims that the growth in human brain size issues from the same source (female preference) as did the growth in peacock's tails: females preferred brainier mates, so brains just kept getting bigger. Most writers would probably content themselves with a more straightforwardly adaptationist story. Peacocks' tails might be dysfunctional, but how could anyone doubt that increased brain size conferred an advantage — indeed, all the advantages conferred by a vastly enhanced intelligence? Thus increased brain size would be selected for regardless of female preference.

But such arguments are highly vulnerable. Why, if big brains were so adaptive *in themselves*, did no previous species select for them at anything like that rate or to anything like that extent? The facts are all the stranger because, while many creatures have no necks and/or no tails, every creature above a pretty low level of development has a brain. If brain growth is so adaptive, it is amazing that this explosive growth happened only once in the hundreds of millions of years during which brains have been evolving.

The view that brain growth is no different from the neck growth of giraffes or the tail growth of peacocks disregards a vast difference in the kinds of change involved. In order to change giraffes' necks, all that had to alter were the genes that controlled the length of a giraffe's neck bones — since giraffes, for all their neck length, have no more bones in their necks than you or I. However, the ingredients of brains are more specialized and diverse than the ingredients of tails and necks. They have to perform a variety of quasi-independent functions (seeing, hearing, smelling, controlling movement, and so on), while the parts that constitute necks and tails have only to sit there. All of the various parts into which brains can be divided are from the very beginning assigned one specialized function or another.[1] Although newspaper advertisements

---

1. Note that this statement is in no sense contradicted by the capacity of the brain to achieve at least partial recovery even after severe trauma. It is not that previously unused sections are co-opted to perform the functions formerly discharged by traumatized areas, but rather that (given the considerable redundancy

for various forms of alleged mind enhancement still contain statements like "We only use 10 percent of our brains," such statements reflect earlier stages of knowledge, in which the functions of many regions of the brain were unknown. Since then, our knowledge of the brain has increased exponentially, yet no one has discovered a single brain area that is initially uncommitted to a specific function.

Thus brains could not possibly have grown with the uninhibited freedom of necks or tails. Additional brain cells had to be committed to one function or another. Indeed, if brain cells had been produced without specific functions, they would hardly have survived the ontogenetic development of the individuals who bore them. Experiments with cats raised in barrels painted exclusively with vertical stripes (Hubel and Wiesel 1962) have shown that brain cells committed to the recognition of horizontal boundaries will atrophy if placed in an environment where there are no horizontal boundaries to be recognized. The same fate would surely have overtaken cells that had no assigned function to begin with.

Moreover, brain growth is subject to a further condition that would have inhibited the development of uncommitted sectors. Brains consist of many cell ensembles, each of which may perform particular functions, but each of which has to cooperate with all the other ensembles in such a way that their owner continuously maintains homeostasis. For this, after all, is what brains are for — to enable their owners to survive in the world, to maximize their opportunities, minimize their dangers, and maintain all conditions that favor the prolongation of life and fertility.

Balance between the growth rates of different brain areas requires, among other things, that those areas be connected with one another so as to ensure maximally efficient cooperation. But the creation of additional cells does not ensure the creation of the necessary additions and changes to the overall wiring pattern of the brain. Indeed, there is reason to believe that these two processes (increase in number of cells,

---

of the brain, and the fact that it remains a dynamic organism throughout life) areas previously adapted for other purposes may be converted so as to discharge those functions. Nor is the statement intended to endorse any kind of simplistic "one structure equals one function" postulate. A given area of the brain may well contribute to a variety of functions, sharing each function with a cohort of other areas.

leading to increases in overall brain size, and changes in the wiring pattern of the brain) are at least partly independent of one another, since, as we shall shortly see, the most dramatic developments in human cognition seem to have occurred without any concomitant increase in brain size.

An increase in brain size has to satisfy a number of constraints—commitment to distinct and specific functions, balance in the growth of quasi-autonomous parts, and satisfactory nervous connections linking new to established areas—that do not have to be satisfied by the growth of other organs. And there is a further constraint that applies to the brain's overall size. The brain has been estimated to consume as much as 20 percent of available oxygen (Hart 1975). Thus any increase in brain size has to pay for itself, so to speak, by providing its owner with some specific compensatory advantage that will at least balance, if not outweigh, the metabolic disadvantages that increased brain size incurs.

Factors such as these make it unwise to treat increases in brain size as being on a par with increases in the size of other organs, hence explicable in the same terms. Furthermore, even the claim that increased brain size must inevitably confer some kind of advantage is far from unproblematic. Just what advantage has brain size bestowed on humans? The usual answer—an enhanced ability to solve problems, or some such formula—simply won't do. All creatures above the level of amoeba have the ability to solve problems, as anyone knows who has ever watched a leaf-cutting ant maneuver a piece of leaf through a gap that is narrower than the leaf. So all creatures would benefit by an enhanced ability to solve problems. In that case, why did no other kind of creature undergo the brain growth that would have conferred this ability? Our unprecedented brain growth must surely have involved the creation of some specific and equally unprecedented capacity.

Language fits the description of such a capacity, and indeed may be the only thing that does. The view that language was the main driving force in the increase of brain size is shared by at least some paleoneurologists, such as Bradshaw (1988) and Falk (1987). However, a majority of scholars in the field of evolution have sought solutions elsewhere.

Often those solutions are unconvincing precisely because they name faculties that we share with other species. Other species have solved complex problems, walked on two legs, used and even made tools, and performed all the other functions that have at one time or another been regarded as uniquely human. Language remains the only significant property unique to humans, despite reiterated claims in the popular press and elsewhere that apes can learn language. A rather different type of evolutionary explanation leans on something which, if it existed, would certainly be unique to humans—an "evolutionary feedback loop" between human brains and human culture (Wills 1993)—which I'll deal with in the following section.

However, there is a third and much stronger reason for rejecting the belief that our big brains *qua* big brains gave us an enhanced intelligence. This reason lies in a series of undisputed facts about hominid evolution.

How the brain grew and how little it could do

The average human brain size is between 1,400 and 1,500 cubic centimeters (Falk 1992:183), representing a range of roughly 1,000 to 2,000 cubic centimeters. This wide variation seems not to correlate with any differences in intelligence. There are people with brains of 2,000 cubic centimeters, like Oliver Cromwell, and there are people with brains of 1,000 cubic centimeters, like Anatole France. Was Oliver twice as smart as Anatole? The question doesn't make sense. Those at the lower end of the scale have as great a command of language and the same kind of mind and consciousness and intelligence as anyone else.

Now mind and consciousness and intelligence of the human variety do not function in a vacuum. They are creative forces that pour forth, in every human society we know of, an inexhaustible stream of both utilitarian and symbolic objects (more in some societies than in others, it is true, but differences in the creativity of different human groups shrink into insignificance when we compare even the least technologically innovative of such groups with all other species, including antecedent hominid species). If intelligence creates such objects, and human intelligence is determined by brain size, we would expect that such objects should have begun to appear when hominid brains first entered the size range of modern human brains—if not before, since the hominid brain had doubled the size of contemporary ape brains well before it entered that range! Indeed, we would predict a gradual and steady increase in the variety and quality of human artifacts, beginning when hominid brains first significantly exceeded the size of contemporary ape brains. Certainly we would have to predict that such differences would have become highly salient by the time the majority of hominids fell within the modern brain-size range.[2]

Indeed, just such a gradualist picture is drawn, even today, by deservedly respected scholars who should know better. For example, Falk (1993:226) states: "The fossil and archaeological record for *Homo* picks up around two million years ago in East Africa. And what a record it is! Brain size 'took off' and subsequently doubled from approximately 700 cubic centimeters to 1400 cubic centimeters. . . . Recorded tool production also accelerated in *Homo*, spanning from initial clunky stone tools to contemporary computer, space and biological engineering." No one reading this passage without prior exposure to the subject would expect that while the increase in brain size was continuous throughout the two million year period, production of everything but the "clunky stone tools" had to wait for the last *two percent* of that period!

But Falk is far from being alone. According to Tobias (1971), "the brain-culture relationship was not confined to one special moment of time. Long-continued increase in size and complexity of the brain was paralleled for probably a couple of million years *by long-continued elaboration and 'complexification' . . . of the culture.* The feedback relationship between the two sets of events is *as indubitable as it was prolonged in time*" (emphasis added). Beliefs such as these have been developed into a theory of gene-culture interaction by Lumsden and Wilson (1983).

Let us look at the realities behind such positions. At a place called Zhoukoudian in northern China, a series of limestone caverns was inhabited by hominids between roughly 500,000 and 200,000 years ago—that is, for about three hundred thousand years, sixty times the entire length of recorded human history (Liu 1985, Jia and Huang 1990). Yet during that entire period, not a single structural improvement was made to those caves; the tiny handful of artifacts produced by its inhabitants underwent no change or improvement; "the people of the caves of Zhoukoudian crouched over their smoky fires, eating their half-cooked bats" (Wills 1993:69) without the slightest trace of the "long-continued elaboration

2. For estimates of brain size increases in the hominid line, see Tobias (1987); and see also Tobias (1964) and Holloway (1966). Day (1986) analyzes in detail the measurements of some of the best-preserved specimens.

and complexification of the culture" that Tobias found so "indubitable." And Zhoukoudian is one of the better documented hominid sites!

Incredible though it may seem in light of Falk's and Tobias's statements (as well as those of many other anthropologists), the fossil record directly refutes those statements. Instead of a steady ascent toward modern, complex culture, we find, for 95 percent of the period, a monotonous, almost flat line. The tools of *Homo habilis*, with a brain-body ratio markedly more favorable than any ape's, are crude in execution and show no clear functional distinctions. The tools of *Homo erectus*, while widely regarded as constituting a significant if relatively slight advance, may not be exactly what they seem.

Davidson and Noble (1993) have proposed that the most celebrated of *erectus* tools, the Achuleian "handaxe," was not a finished tool but rather the core that was left when no more flake tools could be removed from the original flint. Similarly, the more recent (and supposedly more refined) Levallois technique is believed by them to have arisen simply as a means of reshaping an otherwise exhausted core so that more flakes could be removed from it, while Dibble (1987) has shown that the variety of tool forms found in the most recent prehuman stage (the so-called Mousterian industry) can be better explained as due to variable degrees of reduction through wear than to deliberate planning and manufacture. Even if these controversial claims are refuted (a matter we must leave to experts), the range of prehuman artifacts is pathetically narrow, and all such artifacts are purely functional. No object of purely symbolic significance has been discovered from those times.

Yet *erectus* brains first entered the size range of humans around a million and a quarter years ago. By half a million years ago—the start of the Zhoukoudian saga—the brains of most if not all *erectus* members probably fell within the lower half of the modern human range. Worse still for the brain-size/intelligence ratio, by a hundred thousand years ago a subspecies of *erectus*, the Neanderthals, had achieved an average brain size somewhat greater than that of modern humans (various estimates place it between 1,500 and 1,750 cubic centimeters).

While Neanderthals were not the subhuman brutes of popular cartoons, they were not dazzling intellects either. They had adapted to the harsh climate of Ice Age Europe by changing physically, becoming stockier, with a lower surface-to-volume ratio, rather than by producing novel artifacts as their successors, the Cro-Magnons, did. Recent work on their lifestyle and social organization suggests a sharp divide between the two (sub-?)species. Neanderthal tools did not represent a significant advance on those of previous species (Davidson and Noble 1993, Dibble 1987); although they may have been capable of learning from Cro-Magnons, there is no trace of *invention* by Neanderthals, and unlike modern humans they did not follow game herds out onto the steppes of southern Russia (Mellars 1989).

Then along came modern humans, whose brains were smaller and not getting any bigger (human brains have maintained the same size range throughout their existence). Yet after a period of coexistence in Western Europe that may have been as short as a few centuries (Mellars 1989), the Neanderthals were gone. Simultaneously with their demise, our species began to pour forth, at a constantly accelerating pace, the never-ending stream of diverse and novel artifacts, both symbolic and functional, that have produced the largely artifactual world that surrounds us today.

How are we to reconcile facts such as these with the story that brain growth made us smarter? One might claim that there is some magical Brain Size Rubicon which, when crossed, opens up a whole new dimension of intelligence. After all, one might argue, catastrophic changes often issue from the gradual addition of tiny increments: an extra milligram tips the scales; a long, gradual increase in seismic activity leads, at some determinate moment, to a devastating earthquake.

Any such attempt must, however, encounter at least four serious problems. First, while we know why scales tip and earthquakes happen, we do not have the faintest idea why an increase in brain size past a particular point should suddenly open up unprecedented realms of intellectual activity; so the claim is vacuous. Second, since Neanderthal brain size equaled or exceeded human brain size, the claim as stated is simply false. If it were true, Neanderthals would have been smarter than us, and should have caused us to go extinct, rather than vice versa. Third, if brain growth did not yield improved problem solving until it reached a critical mass, then improved problem solving cannot have constituted the selective pressure that fueled brain growth; yet *something* must have selected for brain growth, or it would not have happened in face of the energy cost a larger brain imposes.

The fourth problem is the most interesting, because it hints more directly at a correct solution. We have noted that human brain size increased enormously without any concomitant growth in the overt signs of human intelligence. The other half of the equation is that somewhat in advance of that time when overt signs of human intelligence began to increase exponentially, the human brain ceased to grow! The brain of a Cro-Magnon with a stone-blade kit and the brain of a contemporary human with space shuttles and supercolliders are exactly the same size. To put the contrast as starkly as possible:

Increase in brain size = no increase in intelligence.
No increase in brain size = increase in intelligence.

Although the facts on which these equations are based have been known for some time and are beyond dispute, the paradox that results from them seems, for reasons that remain mysterious, seldom if ever to have been explicitly recognized. Certainly no one, to the best of my knowledge, has made any serious effort to explain it.

There is no way in which the uniquely creative quality of human intelligence—our capacity to adapt the world around us to accord more closely with our own needs and desires—could have been caused merely by the increase in brain size that took place between some apelike ancestor and modern humans. That increase may have been a necessary condition for human intelligence, but could not have been a sufficient condition. There must also have taken place some radical change in the *mode of organization* of the brain, a restructuring that brought within the grasp of our species powers that no other species, not even our immediate ancestors, ever had.

However, while the development of the hominid line cannot be reconciled with the conventional brain-growth story, it is wholly consistent with a story of a very different kind. That story is a play in two acts. In the first act, the growth of a novel, quite specific ability caused the brain to grow, and this ability brought immediate rewards even though it did not immediately turn apes into people. In the second act, a radical reorganization of this larger brain created our species and did away with the need for any subsequent brain-size increase.

An intermediate stage between language and nonlanguage

In order to tell this story, I shall have to consider the evolution of language. For a long time, this topic was a no-no for the people it should have most concerned—professional linguists. To this day there are linguists (e.g., Lightfoot 1991) who openly and unashamedly call for a renewal of the ban which, in 1866, the Linguistic Society of Paris imposed on its members, forbidding them to read, at any of its meetings, any papers on the topic. More recently, a few linguists (Bickerton 1981, 1990; Pinker and Bloom 1990; Newmeyer 1991) have dared to trespass on the forbidden ground, but the topics they have raised are still not deemed worthy of discussion in the pages of professional linguistics journals.[3]

Many linguists have excused themselves from their manifest destiny by pointing to the deficiencies of the fossil record (brains don't fossilize, and still less do words and sentences), but perhaps a more pressing reason for their dereliction of duty lies in their failure to disassemble the object of their inquiry. Evolution, as everyone knows, proceeds in a mosaic fashion, adding increment to increment rather than suddenly conjuring full-fledged organs from the void (Simpson 1953, Mayr 1963). But with a lack of question that must surely amaze practitioners of other disciplines, many linguists have treated language as if it had sprung from Jove's brow—one, entire, unique, and indivisible.

But then linguists have largely ignored the "ape language" experiments (Linden 1975), have regarded pidgins as merely "parasitic upon natural language" (Chomsky 1962),[4] and have insisted on interpreting the language of children under two as continuous with that of older children and under the guidance of the same language faculty, therefore describable in terms of an adult grammar (Bowerman 1973, Brown 1973). A more parsimonious explanation of the striking structural similarities between the utterances of trained apes, pidgin speakers, and children under two is provided in Bickerton (1990). There it is proposed that these utterances represent a way of putting together concepts without any kind of formal structure—a form of expression (quite distinct from,

3. For instance, the Pinker-Bloom article appeared in *Behavioral and Brain Sciences*, the Newmeyer article in *Language and Communication*, a journal which despite its title (or because of the second half of it) few linguists read or contribute to. *Linguistic Inquiry*, in its second year of publication, printed Lieberman and Crelin (1971) on the vocal capacities of Neanderthals, but no comparable work has since appeared in it.

4. To be fair to Chomsky, there is a sense in which pidgins are "parasitic upon natural language" in that they sometimes reflect the word order and other features of the native languages of their speakers (Bickerton 1981, chap. 1). However, their infrastructure is probably separate from, and older than, that of language (Bickerton 1990, chap. 5).

on the one hand, animal calls, and on the other, language) that I refer to as *protolanguage*.

The idea that the utterances of small children do not differ structurally from those of animals has seemed obnoxious to many psycholinguists (e.g., Pinker 1992; but see fellow psycholinguist McNeill 1992 for a more favorable view). Pinker objected on the grounds that I presented a limited (and, he implied, carefully winnowed) corpus to support my claims. My reasons for presenting a limited corpus were simple. I did not wish to bore my readers: whatever your approach, ape language, early-stage pidgins, and the speech of children under two are endlessly, monotonously unstructured, and analytically uninteresting. However, for the benefit of skeptics, Appendix A contains copious samples from all three genres, and I will be interested to hear from any reader who can either (1) write a nontrivial grammar that will account for all examples, or (2) explain what *structural* features differentiate the three genres from one another. As should quickly be apparent, all the data in Appendix A show a total absence of complex sentences, a lack of correlation between function and word order, frequent omission of subcategorized constituents, absence of any mechanism for automatically recovering the reference of phonetically null arguments, and complete or all-but-complete absence of grammatical items—all of the features set forth in Bickerton (1990:122–26) as indicative of the difference between language and protolanguage.

The hypothesis of a protolanguage helps to bridge the otherwise threatening evolutionary gap between a wholly alingual state and the full possession of language as we know it. The linguistic history of the hominid line appears, accordingly, as a two-stage process: first a stage in which there was a lexicon without syntax, then a stage in which infinitely productive mechanisms emerged to create syntax as we know it. If this conclusion is correct, it is a waste of time to look for antecedents of syntax in ancestral species: syntax could not have come into existence until there was a sizable vocabulary whose units could be organized into complex structures. However, it does make sense to seek antecedents of the lexicon among other species.

Antecedents of the lexicon

The roots of the lexicon lie in two things: the capacity to sort objects into categories and the power to form associations between stimuli. Without categories, there can be nothing to attach symbols to, since linguistic symbols, as has been apparent at least since de Saussure (1966, but the material therein dates to the beginning of this century), do not relate directly to objects in the world, but rather to our concepts of the generalized classes to which raw objects belong. Without associations between stimuli (rather than merely between stimulus and response), there would be no way in which symbols could be attached reliably to concepts.

Both categorization and stimulus association are found in a wide variety of species. Creatures at least as dumb as pigeons can categorize objects previously unknown to them (Herrnstein 1988), while probably all vertebrates, as well as some invertebrates, can link stimuli to one another (McPhail 1987). One might not initially think of stimulus association as being a symbolic activity. However, consider Pavlov's most famous experiment in which ringing a bell elicited from dogs the same physical reaction as the presentation of food. It does not seem to stretch the meaning of "symbolism" too far to say that for those dogs the sound of the bell served as a symbol for food. A chain of association had been formed, and it is on just such chains that symbolization depends.[5]

Given categorization and association formation, it becomes possible, not merely for humans, but for a wide range of creatures (a range whose extent has yet to be determined), to attach symbols to categories and to use those symbols correctly, if the appropriate training is provided. (Somehow our remote ancestors managed to do this without training— at that stage, perhaps, the only accomplishment, other than upright walking, that distinguished them from the apes.) To create a true lexicon, one whose constituent items were truly referential, such category labels perhaps needed no more than two additional features: they had to be dissociated from physical manifestations of the concepts they represented, and they had to be stored in a hierarchical structure of meaning relationships potentially capable of representing the entire field of consciousness.

Savage-Rumbaugh (1986) examined carefully the outputs of trained apes in the 1960s and 1970s, and concluded that no more than association was involved: they were not using words referentially. By a series of ingenious experiments she was able to teach her chimpanzee subjects Sherman and Austin to sort symbols into categories such as "tool" or

5. Human use of symbolization requires much more than this, but we are talking now of the origins of symbolic processes, not their culmination.

"food." They thereby acquired (or behaved as if they had acquired) one of the two remaining properties needed for reference: recognition of words as being more than mere object labels, as being abstract units in a hierarchical system with its own network of internal relationships based entirely on meanings.

The fact that other species can accomplish as much as they do with symbolic units strongly suggests that the latent capacities underlying such behavior predate both true language and our own species (although obviously this latency was less widely shared than the mere ability to categorize and form associations). However, there is at least one respect in which use of the symbols taught to other species falls short of human use of words, and that is in the ability to talk about things that are distant in space or time from the speaker.

Terrace (1979) pointed out the infrequency with which trained apes, as opposed to human children, spontaneously initiated exchanges with others. On the rare occasions when apes did initiate conversation, their motive was usually to express their current wants or emotional state, occasionally to point out some feature of the environment. Never, so far as one can tell, were they motivated to volunteer unsolicited information or to recount past events. Yet such functions figure prominently in human verbal exchanges, and indeed are attempted even by small children whose vocabularies are no larger than those of the trained apes.

But how the gulf was bridged between the unbreakable here-and-nowness of animal calls and the unlimited spatiotemporal reference of human language is a question that we cannot yet begin to resolve. It may be that the signs left by other species—footprints, droppings, and so forth—could have served as a bridge between purely associative and fully referential uses. It seems not unreasonable to suppose that a high awareness of, and curiosity about, such traces contributed strongly to hominid survival. Pointing at such a trace while uttering the protoword for a given species could perhaps have been interpreted as meaning "Predator X *was* here, and *may* return"—but here we land squarely within the domain of the just-so story, on which no valid account can be based.

There are, however, good grounds for doubting whether the specific-predator alarm calls of vervets and other species could have served as protowords. If predator calls really function like words do, why didn't acquisition of the capacity to make them lead to a definitive crossing of the Rubicon between saying-how-I-feel and saying-what-I-know, and thus enable creatures to exchange factual information on a variety of other topics? Why did animals capable of giving warnings about preda- tors, and even warnings about different kinds of predator (see Cheney and Seyfarth 1990 on the behavior of vervet monkeys), not then become automatically capable of conveying factual information about different kinds of food, or probable developments in the weather, or the behavior of conspecifics, or other factors that might directly affect their lives? One thing that characterizes language (even protolanguage) and differentiates it from call systems is its open-endedness: once on our side of the word-Rubicon, new symbols can be added indefinitely.

But let us assume, even though this cannot be demonstrated, that a lexicon could have developed on the basis of capacities at least marginally within the genetic and behavioral envelopes of a number of species living around the time of hominid emergence. Given a lexicon, no further capacity seems to be needed to generate propositional utterances. I have commented elsewhere (Bickerton 1990, chap. 5, and Chapter 1, this volume) on the apparent ease with which "linguistically" trained animals have learned to string symbols together. However, there does remain something to be said about what it took for the first linguistic utterance to occur.

What was magic about the magic moment?

In all the literature on language origins, probably nothing has received so much attention as what I have called the "magic moment," when the first meaningful utterance was produced. People have argued endlessly about what kind of utterance it could have been, what might have motivated it, what form it took, and on and on, yet few have thought much about the most crucial features of the magic moment: how the hearers knew that it *was* a meaningful utterance and knew how to respond appropriately.

Think for a moment about the animal call systems that preceded language. These systems, like language, can be broken down into lists of discrete units—lists far shorter, of course, than that of any human language. But the difference is that each of these calls has a specific functional goal: to bring about a particular reaction in the receiver. Thus if one species member utters a certain type of call, other members will react in a predictable way—by running up trees, retreating, trying to mate, or whatever.

Human language differs from this in that the units of language do not have a prescribed function and do not bring about a specific reaction in the receiver. If I were suddenly to exclaim "leopard," for instance, you would not know how to react. Was I warning you of one, or merely pointing one out, or beginning to recite a list of major predators, or solving a crossword puzzle ("can't change spots, in seven letters, ending with d . . .")? You would certainly not have any idea what I might intend you to do. However, if a vervet monkey makes the warning call which some have seen as a word for "leopard," most if not all vervets within earshot will run up trees.

Human language *can* be used to give warnings, or to evoke particular responses. If you are a boxer and I am a referee and I say "Break," you know I am not trying to start a conversation, requesting you to break your opponent's arm, or take five minutes rest. But things referees say to boxers are not typical of normal language use.

The point is not that language *can* be used for certain things, but that animal calls *cannot* be used for anything except controlling or trying to control the behavior of others. This is well known, so why do I devote so much time to it? There are two reasons. First, I want to focus on the problem, far from being solved, of how the first recipient of a linguistic utterance knew that it *was* a linguistic utterance—in other words, knew not to run up a tree. Since hardly anyone seems to have noticed that this *is* a problem, I feel entitled to dwell on it for a moment, even though I don't have any satisfactory solution.

The second and more important reason has to do with the internal workings of the brain. If the vervet leopard call makes vervets run up trees, it presumably does so not because some complex train of thought has been triggered in the vervet's brain—"Aha! There is the leopard call! This can only mean that a leopard is in the vicinity! The logical thing is therefore to run up a tree." Presumably the neurons in the vervet that respond to the leopard call are linked directly to the motor cells that control the behavioral routine of running up the nearest tree.[6]

6. This does *not* mean that the monkey runs up the tree every time it hears the leopard call. Brain functions do not operate through tiny, wholly encapsulated modules that cause inescapable consequences; there is always the possibility that another message, coming from somewhere else in the brain, and triggered by some other aspect of the environment, will inhibit the running-up-a-tree response.

On the other hand, you did not react when I used the word "leopard" because in your brain the areas that store linguistic concepts are not directly linked to any behavioral routine. Language acts as a kind of buffer between ourselves and reality. Within that buffer zone we can take the concept of leopards and turn it around and look at it from a variety of angels without feeling inclined to spear one, run away, or do any other thing.

In probably all other creatures except those that have been trained in symbol use, we may reasonably assume that no such buffer exists. All calls are expected to trigger a response. The level of brain structure at which the creature processes and analyzes *all* its sensory input—its Primary Representational System or PRS (Bickerton 1990)—hooks up directly with output systems. Or, as the saying has it, "Monkey see, monkey do." But if humans see, they may stop, think things over, and maybe do something later, maybe not.

Once a brain starts to represent linguistic symbols, the part where this representation takes place can no longer be coupled with nerve cells that precipitate immediate behavioral consequences. If the representations of linguistic symbols were indeed linked to behavioral responses, there would be no way to distinguish between words and calls. Indeed, immediate responses would defeat the whole purpose of words, just as the absence of such responses would defeat the whole purpose of warning calls.

I have suggested (1990) that one plausible motivation for protolanguage would have been exchange of information about food sources. For creatures like our ancestors of two million years ago, clinging to the ragged edge of survival, extinction could be avoided only by a careful apportioning of resources to food gathering. Only by assessing the relative values of food sources could optimal levels of resource management be achieved. Suppose hominid Ed started to say "Dead mammoth . . ." If the whole clan immediately took off in the direction Ed was pointing, they would never hear him explain that the dead mammoth was several miles distant and was already surrounded by large carnivores. Nor would they hear about the supply of honey that hominid Bud had located less than a mile away with no obvious risk (other than the possibility of getting stung). Given the opportunity, the clan might well decide that a small high-energy food source attainable with little risk and effort would pay off better than a large source requiring considerable risk and a lot of effort. But such decisions could be made only by deliberating at leisure, not plunging immediately into action.

Conversely, if the recipient of a predator alarm call loitered around, waiting to hear what information about the predator might be forthcoming, the consequences would probably be painful and quite possibly fatal for the hominid concerned. It should have been obvious to continuists like Hockett and Ascher (1964) that the antecedent hominid call system and the burgeoning protolanguage had to be kept separate.[7] They were indeed kept separate: alongside language, our species has retained its own call system of screams, shouts, tears, laughter, fist waving, finger giving, and the like. And the vocal part of that system (screams and such) uses wavebands quite distinct from those that language uses.

For the humblest and most primitive protolanguage to start, the units would have had to be represented in areas of the brain not directly linked to areas controlling motor behavior. This was unprecedented in the history of evolution—something that made possible what may have been the most far-reaching event since the emergence of life. Until that moment, ever since the first protozoan wiggled away from an aversive chemical, interactions between organism and environment had been governed by two principles: "If something important happens, do something about it" and "If nothing important happens, save your energy." Now there was an additional principle: "If you see something that might be important, do nothing right now, think about it, and maybe you can do something later on." This third principle would change the world utterly.

What was different about hominid thought

Let's think for a moment about thinking and what thinking is and does. One does not have to read very far to discover that, for a species that spends so much of its time thinking, we don't have much of a handle on the subject. Indeed, some of the best among contemporary minds

7. Hockett and Ascher (1964) elaborated a theory of language origins in which the first propositional utterance consisted of half the call for "food" blended with half the call for "danger." Neither they nor their critics (their paper underwent peer commentary in *Current Anthropology*) seem to have realized that words and calls require quite different reactions, and their work is still treated respectfully in some quarters (for instance, *Current Anthropology* recently reprinted the article in a special issue devoted to ten "landmark" articles that had appeared in the journal over the past few decades).

disagree on the most basic issues. According to Gazzaniga (1985:163), "Thinking, even thinking simply, is unique to man." According to Patricia Churchland, however, "The octopi who unscrew mason jars to get the food inside, the macaques who wash their sandy potatoes in the sea, and the rooks who drop stones on would-be invaders all display a solution that is in some degree intelligent" (1986:388). Which is right? Both, of course. The conflict arises only because of a failure to make the essential distinction between what one might call *on-line thinking* and *off-line thinking*.[8]

Most creatures practice on-line thinking. Stretching a point, one might even claim that the bacterium that retreats from or advances toward a trace chemical in the water through which it swims (depending on whether the chemical is poisonous or nutritious to it) has achieved "a solution . . . in some degree intelligent"—a dumb bacterium could have forged ahead and gotten burned—although the degree involved must be the lowest possible one. Certainly, the lizard that monitors a fly's activity and decides (quite unconsciously, of course) how closely it dare approach before pouncing, the provisioning wasp that uses landmarks and an internalized map of space to locate the offspring that it has scattered in holes in the ground, or the bat that processes sonar echoes from a violently evading moth at a speed that only our most recent technology can equal—these are all engaged in some form of mental computation to which it would seem churlish to deny the name of thought (Griffin 1992). But these thinking processes, no less than the rarer, more striking, and more original examples cited by Churchland, are all done on-line, while the animal concerned is engaged in the processes of food gathering, prey locating, intruder repelling, or whatever.

Just as calls are environmentally triggered and in turn trigger a response, so must be the identifications of other species on which calls are based: see a member of another species and you flee it, drive it away, eat it, or ignore it, depending on what species you determine it to be. You do not, if you value your evolutionary future, go into a long dialogue

8. The distinction made here is akin to the on-line/off-line distinction made by Ingvar (1990), Tyler (1992), and others in referring to what some neuropsychologists describe as *implicit tasks* (which do not require conscious awareness on the part of the subject) as opposed to *explicit tasks* (which do require such awareness). However, the terms are usually used only in the context of experimental tasks—not, as here, over thinking as a whole.

with yourself on whether to do anything about it, and if so, what. Any thinking system that did this would have been selected against, and fast, by evolution. To enjoy the luxury of off-line thinking, you need a reasonable margin of safety between you and extinction.

So far as we know (and one would not want to rule out the possibility that there may still be surprises in store for us), only humans are capable of this luxury. Only humans can work on problems that do not immediately confront them (but might, at some time in the future); only humans can assemble fragments of information to form a pattern that they can later act upon without having to wait on that great but unpunctual teacher, experience. As will be shown in the next chapter, it is this capacity for off-line thinking, rather than some mysterious extra power of logic or rationality or computational skill possessed by human thinking, that endows our species with its unique and uniquely creative intelligence. But off-line thinking was impossible until there existed areas of the brain where new information could be processed without needing to be triggered by environmental input and without invoking immediate behavioral consequences.

Protolanguage could have created—or rather, would have had to create—a potential workspace for off-line thinking. First, words have to be represented in the brain, somewhere, somehow. Second, such representations must be kept free of direct contact with motor centers, if inappropriate reactions to words (reactions of the type appropriate to calls) are to be avoided. However, let us also consider a slightly different scenario. Let us suppose that, initially at least, and despite the arguments raised earlier against the improbability of this, the brain did expand with no good reason for doing so. Or perhaps there was some functional motivation; perhaps a larger brain was able to develop because its venous system served as a radiator to dissipate body heat, as suggested by Falk (1990). Note that Falk explicitly dissociates herself from the idea that the venous system's cooling role *caused* brain expansion; it merely *allowed* expansion.

Once this development had begun, the new areas might have been "colonized" by ensembles of cells converting adjacent cells into functional copies of themselves along lines suggested, very plausibly, by Calvin (1993). This could conceivably have created multiple representations of whatever was already in the PRS. Moreover, since these new areas would not yet have established behavior-triggering links with motor regions, the representations they contained could have provided both the materials and the kind of environment required for off-line thinking. Protolanguage would then have developed as soon as links were formed between the new areas and those that controlled the vocal organs.

One or two things about this alternative are quite appealing. First, it places the origins of language even more firmly in purely representational (instead of communicational) developments than a "protolanguage first" approach does. Second, it would neatly solve the problem of how the second hominid understood the first meaningful statement by the first hominid. If the first hominid's utterance simply replicated in expressive form the thought that already happened to be passing through the second hominid's mind, no problem would arise—the second hominid would hardly misinterpret the utterance as a call to immediate action.

However, this alternative has problems of its own. The unlikelihood of random unmotivated brain enlargement has already been mentioned. A more subtle problem lies in the nature of the representational process itself.

Recent experiments have confirmed the existence in the human brain of multiple representations of "the same" concept. For instance, Hart and Gordon (1992) report on the case of a subject, K.R., who as a result of brain damage lost the ability to name or describe animals, although she was able to assemble drawings of these same animals when cut-up pictures were presented to her. The authors' conclusions merit quotation at some length: "This demonstration of two distinct representational systems, one subserving visually based knowledge and one for language-based knowledge, is prima facie evidence for a distinction already suggested by behavioral and neuroanatomic data. But K.R.'s data allow us to go beyond this general specification, claiming that there is, in some cases, a duplication of some types of knowledge for physical attributes across the two systems. . . . [N]ormally there is a dual representation for visual physical attributes, one visually based and one language-based. . . . [T]he language system must contain multiple subdomains of knowledge representation (such as visual physical attributes) functionally, and in some sense anatomically, distinguishable." This and similar cases confirm empirically the distinction, made on theoretical grounds in Bickerton (1990), between nonlinguistic (primary) and linguistic (secondary) representational systems.

However, when viewed in the context of the evolution of language, Hart and Gordon's findings raise interesting questions. Could two distinct systems have come into existence simply because cells that underlay representations in the first system colonized and usurped the functions of adjacent cells? Or would such a process have produced stronger (perhaps, redundantly stronger) primary representations? This is an empirical question. If the answer is positive, the alternative scenario for the creation of an off-line thinking workspace might prove viable; otherwise not.

At least one line of argument seems to go against the alternative scenario. In the previous chapter it was shown that when we are "thinking in images" about the cat that sat on the mat, the "images" that come to us are not of particular mats or particular cats, but rather of "just a cat" and "just a mat" (those spoilsport readers who at this stage say things like, "Well, *you* might have been, but *I* was thinking of my favorite Siamese on my Aubusson" are hereby required to tell what particular cats or mats they think of when "imaging" the sentence "No cat sat on any mat"). But in the whole of nature there is nothing that is "just a cat" or "just a mat"—nothing, that is, except the words *cat* and *mat*, and sketches like that in Figure 2.1, which are produced exclusively by a species that has words.[9]

Indeed, if it is to be any use at all, a vocabulary cannot possibly mark all the particularities of objects that our senses reveal to us. If we are to think off-line in any general sort of way (rather than on-line about the particular things that momentarily happen to confront us), we have to boil down the Jamesian "buzzing, blooming confusion" of sensory experience into a much thinner gruel. The fact that pigeons (and all "higher" species) can sort things into categories does not mean that their "conceptual structure" (Jackendoff 1987) must contain representations of abstract categories as such—representations that they can manipulate

---

9. It is very significant that while apes have produced "abstract" paintings (and at least one has even sold some to nonrelatives, a better track record than Van Gogh's), no ape has yet been found that can draw representationally *at all*, let alone at the level of the average three-year-old human. Apes can hardly plead lack of manual dexterity for this deficit. To be able to draw the kinds of objects that small children (and we average artistically challenged adults) draw, one first has to have highly stereotyped images of those objects—images that abstract away from their countless particularities in just the way that words do.

Figure 2.1
"Just a cat"

in thought. That's an assumption for which there is no evidence whatsoever. But a species that uses words must have representations of abstract categories to base those words upon, and the most parsimonious proposal is that, without words, such categories could not have been formed in the first place. If our ancestors had not begun to acquire words, what else could have motivated these abstract representations?

Whether words begat abstract representations, or abstract representations made words possible, is a purely empirical issue, unlikely to be clarified until we better understand how the brain works to produce language, thought, and action. Yet whichever scenario is correct, a gradually increasing protolanguage remains the single most plausible engine for the maintenance of brain expansion over the lifetime of *erectus*. Suppose the contrary: suppose the brain grew and developed as a machine not for language but for off-line thinking, with protolanguage and subsequent language resulting as mere spin-offs, the purely derivative and communicational devices that the conventional wisdom holds them to be. What would the consequence be for a coherent evolutionary story?

We would totally lose our reasoned explanation for the peculiar progress of the hominid line: a long period of semistagnation through the lifetimes of *habilis* and *erectus*, followed by an explosion of clearly intelligent behavior shortly after the emergence of our own species. We would have no way of explaining why the kind of off-line thinking that has brought us so quickly to our current dominance over other species did not begin much earlier, and did not shower our remote ancestors with its fruits of technological progress. No Rubicon of thinking whose crossing could have led to this staggering change in human fortune seems half as convincing as the move from an unstructured, restricted, pidginlike protolanguage to the syntactically structured, infinitely recursive richness of true language.

However, if brain growth came about simply to store and sort the vastly increased amounts of information that would be made available by a protolanguage, we can account for why brains got so much bigger without, apparently, any significant increment in intelligence. Consider the vast amount of lore that is stored in the collective memories of traditional societies: the uses of herbs, the habits of animals, aphorisms about human behavior, detailed knowledge of the spatial environment, anecdotes, old wives' tales, legends, and myths—a huge jumbled attic of truths and falsehoods, all accepted equally and passively, some of it false or useless but much of it likely to be of practical application at one time or another.

Societies like that don't last forever in our species and usually don't last very long. Humans are forever jiggling the pattern, putting odd and unexpected bits together, drawing surprising inferences (and acting on them, of course). But if you can imagine the most hidebound traditional society you know and then imagine it going on, generation after generation, millennium after millennium, with no changes whatsoever, that is perhaps the nearest one can get to feeling what life was like in *erectus* times. These ancestors of ours were not stupid, and they learned a lot, far more than any previous species had done. And they were, in principle, capable of off-line thinking. They surely had the workspace for it.

But having a workspace for something does not mean that you automatically get to make full use of that workspace. As noted earlier in this chapter, off-line thinking is a luxury that carries considerable risks. To our remote ancestors, subject to predation from a number of species, constantly searching for food over a sparse and seasonally changing terrain, those risks would have loomed large, and the opportunities for practicing off-line thinking would have been correspondingly diminished. Moreover, in a tribal lifestyle whose constant, unavoidable intimacies may be all but unimaginable to the solitary, anomic intellectuals of today, moments of relaxation from the fight for survival would have been filled with the exigencies of social life, the struggle to maintain or improve one's place in the pecking order, the forging of alliances and the circumvention of the plots of rivals and enemies.

Nor was this all. In Bickerton (1990) I suggested a further reason why the workspace for off-line thinking could not have been fully utilized until the development of language as we know it. The possession of a protolanguage did not provide an instrument flexible enough to exploit the possibilities of off-line thinking to the full. Consider the *kind* of thinking that must have been necessary before a novel type of artifact could even begin to be produced. Such imaginative thinking is far more dependent on language than the kind of thinking most commonly invoked in language origins studies (e.g., by many contributors to Gibson and Ingold 1993)—the kind of thinking necessarily involved in the manufacture of already invented tools or the teaching of existing tool technology. Consider what would have been required to produce the first harpoon or barbed arrow. Simple though such objects may seem to us now, they were not thought of by any hominid species prior to our own. In order to invent them, you first had to imagine what effect they might have. You had to be able to build whole sequences of conjectural events, something along the lines of: "If I took this arrow and replaced its simple point with something that also pointed the other way, then if it hit a beast and the beast jumped about, as beasts tend to do when they are hit, the arrow would not be able to fall out of the beast as our present arrows so often do, and thus even if the arrow did not kill the beast immediately, it would keep the wound open and the beast would go on losing blood until it became so weak that I could capture it."

I'm not suggesting that these thoughts in anything like this specific form necessarily flitted through some Cro-Magnon brain. However, it would hardly occur to anyone to put a barb on a projectile without first constructing something roughly equivalent to the chain of reasoning I just described. The right concepts have to be assembled in the right way, whether the output is spoken or remains private. What ways of assembling those concepts are there, other than the ways utilized by syntax? No coherent alternative has been suggested. But it is absurd to suppose that in such a chain of reasoning the units will simply fall into place of their own accord. To think that kind of thought, exactly the same relations have to be made as are made in syntax: Agents have to be seen as performing actions, Patients as suffering them, and most crucial of all, logical connections such as cause-and-effect, if . . . then, not . . . unless, and so forth have to be set up, which in turn requires a syntactic mechanism of some form. Are those who would claim separation between language and off-line thought going to claim that the latter has a syntax of its own, separate and different from that of language?

If syntax is indeed the Rubicon between thought as we know it and more primitive ways of thought, and if syntax is peculiar to our species (we are surely the only living species that has it), we have a simple and straightforward explanation for the two most shocking facts of human evolution: that our ancestors stagnated so long despite their ever-growing brains, and that human culture grew exponentially only *after* the brain had ceased to grow.

Brains got bigger because protolanguage created bigger brains and yielded an immediate adaptive payoff in terms of survival: it became possible to warn of more remote dangers, to pool useful information, to plan foraging activities, and the like. But that payoff did not include cultural acceleration, because protolanguage—a slow, clumsy, ad hoc stringing together of symbols—would not support the kind of thinking that led to radical innovation (obviously, off-line thinking can be innovative or noninnovative). With no reliable syntax, there was no way of constructing complex propositions. If complex propositions (cause-and-effect, if . . . then, not . . . unless) could not be constructed, there was no escape out of "doing things the way we always did, but a bit better" into "doing things in ways no one thought of before." So for all their ever-growing brains, brains that grew in the end to a size greater than our own, hominids found no escape from cultural stagnation.

In short, protolanguage enabled prehuman hominids to function more efficiently *as* prehuman hominids, but it didn't and couldn't make them human. It did not allow them to turn today's imagination into tomorrow's fact. But it is just this power to transform imagination into fact that distinguishes human behavior from that of our ancestral species, and indeed from that of all other species. It is exactly what enables us to change our behavior, or invent vast ranges of new behavior, practically overnight, with no concomitant genetic changes, whereas the behaviors of all other species are contained within quite narrow limits, genetically specified envelopes, that make any radical behavioral change contingent upon an equally radical genetic change.

But this power to turn imagination into fact could not have come from any increase in brain size; as we have seen, the hominid brain had even shrunk somewhat before that power made itself manifest. What enabled us to reorganize our lives therefore can only have been some change in the internal structure of the brain, rather than in its size or shape.

The origins of syntax

So how could syntax have come about? If the presence of syntax is what distinguishes language from protolanguage, it may be helpful to review some of the things that must have happened for protolanguage to become language. The random stringing together of words must have been replaced by their arrangement into hierarchical tree structures. The random omission of words essential in a discourse (leaving the hearer to infer them from context) must have been replaced by their obligatory insertion, except where automatic computational procedures (of the kind that tell us who will be the employer and who the employee in *Bill has found someone to work for*) determine the reference of the missing elements. The range of complex substructures brought into being by this hierarchization and these computational procedures would have begun to be signaled by abstract markers like *the, a, this, that* (as in "that boy"), *that* (as in "I think that . . ."), *that* (as in "The man that . . ."), *for, to, by, of, at, because, although, unless*—words of a type wholly unknown in protolanguage.[10]

Such things as rules for recovery of meaning and abstract, nonreferential forms are just a couple of the distinctive *and universal* aspects of human language that render wholly implausible the idea that language could have been constructed before the dawn of history by clever humans in the process of achieving some "higher" representational purpose. Yet there are still many who hold to this view, for instance Donald

---

10. The items in this paragraph are selected, of course, for illustration only. Obviously many languages do not have equivalents of the particular English terms chosen here. But all languages have forms with similarly abstract functions. There is no human language that consists entirely of content-words, or that lacks a list of dozens, if not hundreds, of nonreferential items such as are shown here.

(1991:216), who claims, "Words and sentences, lexicons and grammars, would have become necessary evils, tools that had to be invented to achieve this higher representational goal. . . . Above all, language was a public, collective invention." Here again we encounter the "if viewed from a distance" syndrome mentioned in the previous chapter: the nearer we get to the very specific types of complexity that language evinces, the harder it becomes to believe that those quirky complexities could have sprung from anything one could reasonably call invention or creation. But lest the reader conclude that the only argument for the biological nature of syntax is what Dawkins (1986) called the "argument from personal incredulity," consider the following.

If syntax is an invention, like other human inventions (agriculture, the wheel, ballistic weapons, representational art, and so forth), it forms a part of human culture. What is most striking about human culture is the immense variety that exists, synchronically as well as diachronically, within the human species. Take an *erectus* community from Africa a million years ago and one from China, Spain, or Indonesia a couple of hundred thousand years ago, and you will find that few if any significant cultural differences distinguish them. But among contemporary humans you can find every type and degree of culture, from primitive hunters and gatherers with toolkits little more sophisticated than those of Cro-Magnon, to modern technological societies with computers, television, jet planes, and an endless array of similar gadgets. You can find extreme simplicity, extreme complexity, and pretty well every intermediate stage.

When you turn to human language, the contrast is absolute. No one can claim that any of the five thousand or so human languages is more advanced or more developed or more complex than any other. True, nonprofessionals may opine that some languages (e.g., English, Chinese) are simpler or have less grammar than others, but ironically, even on these terms the simplest languages turn out to belong not to the least developed but to the most advanced and complex cultures. In fact, what seems like simplicity in one area of a language's grammar will always be compensated for by complexity in another, so that an approximate equality of all languages is assured. All human languages can express the same range of experience and all have similar (and similarly complex) devices for doing so.

Is this what one would predict if language were indeed an invention, part of culture? Absolutely not. One would expect to find "primitive" peoples with "primitive" languages, "advanced" societies with "advanced" languages, and a whole spectrum of language types in between, just as we do with cultural manifestations in general. We do not. Instead we find variation confined to the most superficial levels of language, the choice of particular words to express concepts common to all languages and the choice of sounds (out of a fixed repertoire of human speech sounds containing less than a hundred units) that give physical expression to those words.

Consider too the issues raised by human dispersion. Until a couple of centuries ago, native Australians had been separated from the rest of the species for around fifty thousand years. However, Australian languages have the same forms of organization as all other languages. Suppose language really was a cultural invention: it must thus have been invented prior to the separation of Australians from the rest of the species.[11] But if the essential structure of language was invented more than fifty thousand years ago, how is it that our restless minds have not changed its structure anywhere, have not modified it and improved on it to the widely varying extent that all other human inventions have been modified or improved upon over the last fifty millennia?

Thus there seems no viable alternative to concluding that syntax has a specific neural substrate laid down at some stage prior to those last fifty millennia, most probably at the time when anatomically modern humans emerged as a separate species. But how exactly could such a substrate have arisen?

Some linguists who have written recently on language evolution (e.g., Pinker and Bloom 1990, Newmeyer 1991) see the emergence of syntax as a gradual process, spread out over at least several hundred thousand years (both accounts get a little vague when it comes to tying syntactic developments to specific phases of hominid evolution). Something similar (and similarly vague) was proposed in Bickerton (1981). In Bickerton (1990),

11. I am assuming that the separation of Australians from the rest of the species was the first such permanent separation. It may be that Australia underwent one or more subsequent waves of immigration at a somewhat later date. However, this would not affect the argument. The native inhabitants of America arrived there over ten thousand years ago, at a time when the technological diversification of cultures had not yet begun, and were not contacted by any other groups until relatively recent times. But again, the languages of America all follow the universal pattern, whereas cultural levels within America diversified radically.

however, it was claimed that the development from protolanguage to true language, via the emergence of syntax, was a catastrophic event, occurring within the first few generations of the species *Homo sapiens sapiens*. What had happened in the intervening nine years to change my mind?

Only between these two dates did I become aware that the theory of punctuated equilibrium (Eldredge and Gould 1972) was a respectable alternative to neo-Darwinian gradualist orthodoxy. Although many evolutionary developments come about very gradually, through a slow-building mosaic of cumulative adaptations, not all of them do. There is also the possibility, in small populations, of very rapid cascades of change. In many evolutionary lines, what we see is not smooth, gradual change spread out evenly over countless millennia, but rather countless millennia of stagnation, followed by quite sudden shifts to new plateaux of stability.

The similarity between this scenario and the story told by the human fossil record struck me immediately. Here were the Falks and Tobiases interpreting that record, telling us that what had happened was indeed just the kind of steady climb up the hills of cultural development that neo-Darwinian gradualism had predicted. And there was the fossil record itself, telling us that nothing of the kind had happened; that *Homo habilis* had gone through a species lifetime without any significant change, that *erectus*, emerging abruptly with a slightly better toolkit, had in turn stagnated for a million and a half years, and that our own species then burst upon the scene with a still incomplete torrent of spectacular innovations—innovations different not just in quantity but in kind from all the innovations of preceding species. If this wasn't punctuated equilibrium, what was it?

In the next chapter we will look at how language liberated human thought from the constraints placed upon animal thought. It should become apparent (if it hasn't already) that if you have anything approximating human language, you have a tool for thinking that has enormous power: a tool not for just any old thinking, but specifically for the kind of thinking that changes your technology and your culture, that gives you fishhooks, coracles, harpoons, game traps, domestic animals, houses, bridges, wheels. Is it conceivable that a group of hominids could have had 65 percent of modern human language or 85 percent of modern human language and still gone on, millennia after millennia, with zero percent change in the way they lived?

Note, please, that this is not the familiar anti-evolutionary argument: What use was 5 percent of an eye? (The answer is, of course: A lot more than 2 percent of an eye!) If you *could* have had 65 percent of language (we're coming to that in a moment), it would have been very useful to *erectus*. So useful that they would hardly have sat for 0.3 million years in the drafty, smoky caves of Zhoukoudian, cooking bats over smoldering embers and waiting for the caves to fill up with their own garbage. So useful that the absence of any significant improvement in the lives of our ancestral species naturally suggests that they couldn't have had 65 percent, or 50 percent, or even 30 percent of human language.

I want to make this argument very clearly because it represents the stronger prong of a two-pronged argument that is sometimes trivialized by looking only at its weaker prong. Its weaker prong is the argument, What else but the emergence of language could have caused the cultural explosion of the last forty or fifty thousand years? The trouble with "What else?" arguments is that someone can say, "Well, *I* can think of something else," and even if the something else sounds pretty unlikely, there is no way you can prove it impossible.

But now look at the other prong. The oldest members of our own species that we can be sure of, those found at the mouth of the Klasies River in South Africa (Binford 1984), are little more than a hundred thousand years old. By about fifty thousand years ago our species had spread over most of Asia, Africa, and Australia. In a few thousand years they wrested control of Europe from the apparently much better adapted Neanderthals and sent them into extinction. Since that time, culture has never ceased its acceleration. We're talking about a species that has language—the only one that we know has language. Would a species with language remotely like ours have been content just to use language for socializing, sitting round smoky fires and gossiping, telling tales, singing? You may say that some human groups have done little more than that with it. True, but not *all* human groups, and even the least technological of modern human groups would leave behind it a fossil store that would put *erectus* to shame. If language as we know it had been developing in *erectus* times, is it in any way plausible to suppose that *no* hominid group, over hundreds of thousands of years, would have made *any* significant cultural or technological innovation? A gradual growth of language would argue for an equally gradual growth in human culture—but such gradual growth never took place.

Now let's look at a quite different kind of argument. If there had existed some intermediate stages between protolanguage and true language, it would not seem unreasonable to expect traces of such stages to surface somewhere in the wide range of regional and social varieties, in restricted codes, professional jargons and play languages (like pig latin), in the varying styles of different levels of discourse, in "language birth" (the pidgin-into-creole cycle) or "language death" (the reduced and mangled forms one finds often in the last handful of speakers of a disappearing language), in the course of language development among children, or in the countless types of language distortion that may result from drugs, alcohol, fatigue, strokes, psychosis or head injuries, not to mention dysphasias and abnormal developmental syndromes. If any intermediate stages had existed, surely in this rich soup of linguistic diversity, some hints of such a stage might be found?

We do find varieties, such as the early stages of pidgins, or the earliest stages of language acquisition (whether first or second), or what is known as "home sign" among the deaf, or the speech or signing of those who have been deprived of language during the critical period for acquisition, such as Genie (Curtiss 1977) or Chelsea (Curtiss 1988), or the speech of some (not all) victims of mental retardation, that clearly differ markedly from full human language. But all varieties betray the distinguishing marks of protolanguage: the absence of hierarchical structure, the absence of grammatical items, the random absence of required elements of discourse, the lack of any automatic means for recovering the meaning of such "missing" elements, the absence of recursive mechanisms for expanding phrases and clauses and sentences. We find the same beadlike stringing together of small numbers of content words (words that refer directly to entities or actions, such as "dog" or "go," as opposed to grammatical items such as "to" or "was"), the same inability to combine these into any kind of complex sentence, the same slow rate of utterance, the same pauses and hesitations as if even to achieve this low linguistic level cost the speaker a far greater effort than the production of true language costs a normal speaker. In other words, we find protolanguage; and between protolanguage and language, we find nothing.

Some readers may think we should not expect to find anything. In the lovely butterfly, what trace is there of the ugly caterpillar that preceded it? Perhaps intermediate forms simply self-destructed when true language emerged. But what could such intermediate forms have looked like?

"Grammars of intermediate complexity are easy to imagine," claims Steven Pinker (1993:366). True, in the same way that it's easy to imagine Dennett's purple cow. It is only when you wonder what its horns were like, which way it was looking, and so forth, that the job starts to seem more tricky. Premack (1985) suggested two intermediate systems, and I explained at the time (Bickerton 1986) why neither would work; since Premack didn't try to defend them in his reply (Premack 1986), I won't repeat that here. Pinker suggests that such intermediate languages "could have symbols with a narrower range, rules that are less reliably applied, modules with fewer rules." Could they? If symbols had a narrower range, you would need more symbols to do the same amount of work, and what is less complex about that? If rules are less reliably applied, you have to think when you speak about whether to apply them, and when you listen about whether they have been applied; if you have to put so much time and effort into it, what is less complex about that?

As for fewer rules, that sounds fine till you start to think about it. What rules? Chomsky's theory of language, the "principles and parameters" model of generative grammar (Chomsky 1981, 1986), has only one rule, "Move alpha," which means move anything anywhere. You could hardly have fewer rules than that. True, but that rule (which by itself would lead to an appalling mishmash of word salad) is constrained by a number of principles, so perhaps Pinker meant "fewer principles." Well maybe, but which? Subjacency? Subjacency is a principle limiting the distance that can separate, say, a question word like *what* from the "missing" constituent to which it's related (like the object of *eat* in *What did you want to eat?*). If it were not for subjacency you could get questions like *What after Bill had gone out and done the shopping did he come home, play the piano for a while, and then go out without waiting to eat?* You just cannot have questions like that, and you could not process them if you did. Is that Pinker's "grammar of intermediate complexity"? And if he wouldn't scrap *that* rule or principle, which ones *would* he scrap?

To be convincing, any candidate for an intermediate stage would have to meet certain constraints: it should constitute a viable system, it should not buy ease for the speaker at the price of difficulty for the hearer, or vice versa, and it should be capable of conversion into language-as-we-know-it by a series of logical and natural developments. Anything short of this is mere hand waving.

Another problem for gradualism arises from what might seem the strongest point in its favor: the workings of natural selection. Both the Pinker-Bloom (1990) and Newmeyer (1991) arguments for the gradual evolution of language are based in large part on natural selection, which is what generally drives the evolution of complex mechanisms from simpler ones—what built wings out of cooling devices or eyes out of simple light-sensitive cells. A tiny improvement in cell or cooling device benefits the creature that undergoes it, its life is prolonged, its offspring multiply, its genes spread through the gene pool, and the tiny improvement serves as a launchpad for further tiny improvements. So what could possibly be wrong with this well-established story when the complex mechanism happens to be language?

The problem lies in determining what selective pressure(s) would have driven the expansion of an already existing (yet still not fully human) form of language. Typical selective pressures are changes in climate and vegetation, emergence of a new predator, prey, or competitor species, fluctuations in the numbers of such species, changes in the attack or defense capabilities of existing prey and predators or the strategies of existing competitors, or the vacation of adjacent niches due to the extinction of competitors. Few of these pressures seem to have strongly affected our ancestors, and any that did were hardly of a type that would select for more complex language. Pinker and Bloom, along with Newmeyer, therefore pick on the single novel factor in the whole situation—competition between human groups. Such competition, they argue, would surely have led to a beneficial spiral of improvement, as individuals with better language capacities outmaneuvered their less proficient clanspersons, and as groups with better language capacities outmaneuvered groups that were less linguistically endowed.

We should note that by using this argument these writers implicitly support the position of the present volume regarding the relation between language and thought. They are not arguing that one group overcame another by *talking* better; they are arguing that as a result of *talking* better, one group overcame another by *thinking* better. Elsewhere, Pinker (1992; 1993, chap. 3) has stated his opinion that we think in something called "mentalese," which we then simply translate into language. But this is surely incompatible with Pinker and Bloom (1990):

if the later Pinker is right, only an improvement in their mentalese could have given some individuals or groups the edge over others, and there would have been no selective pressure for language. And if one were then to argue that an improvement in mentalese must cause a concomitant improvement in the language that expressed it, one would have arrived very close to the argument that will be developed in the next chapter: that mentalese, or "the language of thought," is just a fancy name for Language-with-a-big-L, the faculty of which all of the world's many spoken and signed languages are merely local expressions.

But what is wrong with assuming that there *were* gradual and steady improvements in *something*—whether mentalese or language—and that these improvements were driven by human competition? There are at least two serious problems here. The first is that there is no evidence of any competition between human *groups* in the period between the emergence of our species and the isolation of Australians (remember that language must have perfected itself by the latter date, otherwise Australian languages would show significant differences from languages elsewhere in the world—and they do not). For that matter, there is no evidence of competition between *erectus* groups.

The trouble lies in a back-projection of current society into prehistoric times. Why are all modern human groups competitive? Because they all have neighbors, and as long as neighbors have to exploit finite resources, they will compete for those resources. But *erectus* spread into a vacuum inhabited only by less successful hominid or prehominid groups, and our own species spread into a vacuum inhabited only by *erectus*. To get some of the flavor of those times, we need only go back as far as the settlement of the American West, where hardy pioneers (genetically indistinguishable from their ancestors who had spread into Asia ninety thousand years earlier) moved until they could no longer see the smoke from their neighbor's hearth before settling, and picked up stakes again when the smoke of new neighbors began to appear on their horizons. True, they competed with the native Americans who had got there first, but they did not compete with one another—at least, not until the West was won, and cattlemen and sheepmen faced off over land and water resources that had suddenly become limited. When an early human group split up or became too large for its habitat, why would its former members have stayed to struggle alongside one another when there were fertile, empty valleys over the hill?

Doubtless there was competition *within* groups, as there has always been. But if (as seems likely) the early part of the human saga was a slow but steady diaspora, how would any improvement of language *within* a group have been transmitted to other groups? If the view of human prehistory in the previous paragraph is anywhere near correct, there was negligible gene flow between human groups from the inception of the species until relatively recent times. Indeed, the wide range of phenotypic differences that developed so rapidly in our species— plump, stocky Eskimos, beanpole Masai, tiny pygmies, bleached sub-arctic dwellers and black tropical ones—strongly support this picture of negligible gene flow.

The second problem with the "selective pressure" argument for gradualism in language development lies in what, exactly, would have ben selected for, and why. This brings us back to the problem of reconstructing possible intermediate stages of language development, under the constraint that each hypothesized stage must constitute a viable system. Pinker and Bloom (1990) try to deal with this problem by assuming that the syntactic mechanism consists of several parts; they further assume (implicitly: they make no attempt to work out what an intermediate system would have been like) that these parts can be dissociated from one another and that the absence of a part would still have left a viable system.

In assuming that the syntactic mechanism consists of several quasi-independent modules, Pinker and Bloom are merely following Chomsky, whose most recent theory involves exactly this kind of description of syntax.[12] Accordingly we cannot really evaluate their proposals without considering how plausible, in light of evolutionary and other evidence, Chomsky's model is.

Evolution, neurology, and the Chomskyan paradigm

Chomsky and his followers will ask, at this stage, why anyone would start talking about evolutionary plausibility when we know so little about

---

12. Chomsky is currently engaged in working out a refinement of this model (see Chomsky 1993) which will apparently reduce the number of modules required by syntax, making it possible to derive some modules from others. It cannot be too strongly emphasized that any move in this direction substantially narrows the gap between Chomskyan theory and what is proposed here, and makes the former much more compatible with the evidence surveyed in the next section.

human evolution, so little about the phylogeny, structure, and functioning of the human brain, and so much about language. Surely the shoemaker should stick to his last, the syntactician to his syntax. If a theory constitutes the best explanation of syntax that we have, it is the best theory, and nothing from any other domain of knowledge can legitimately make us change it. Still less can anything from other domains refute it.

One can grant all of this, as I do, and still take a completely different approach. It is true that whatever biological adaptation produced language has to be able to produce all the effects that have been observed by syntacticians over the last few decades of intensive research. It is true that right now we have little if any idea how these effects are achieved by the human brain, and probably less about how they could have evolved. But *sooner or later* science will have to confront the two closely related problems of how syntax evolved and how syntax is executed by the brain. We can decide that these problems are insoluble, or that it is too early to begin dealing with them. But science does not progress by waiting for new knowledge to come in and for problems to solve themselves. Science progresses by leaping far ahead of what is known, by forming speculative hypotheses and then determining what facts need to be discovered in order to test those hypotheses. It is therefore equally legitimate to choose a third course, and to start tackling the problems right away. Which of these three decisions we make is not a matter of fact, or of logic, but simply a matter of temperament.

The sooner we start building bridges between the study of language, on the one hand, and studies of human evolution and human neurology on the other, the better. To be sure, our earliest proposals on the subject will probably be naïve and misguided. This does not matter as long as we realize that those proposals are first approximations that will have to be revised countless times. Nothing cures proposals of their naïveté and misguidedness quicker than open dialogue between all professionals concerned with the relevant issues.

From this standpoint, let us see how plausible a modular theory of syntax seems in terms of evolution and the neural substrate. Pinker and Bloom (1990) suggest that such a theory conforms well with a scenario of evolutionary gradualness, since modules could have developed independently at different times. Thus some groups might have had a grammar with the constraints of the subjacency principle discussed above, and some might have had a grammar that lacked those constraints. But what adaptive advantage would subjacency provide? Are we to imagine that while members of Group A were hearing, understanding, and competently executing instructions like *Go get the cache of handaxes that Og hid under the big boulder yesterday,* members of Group B stood around scratching their heads while trying to process *Go get the cache of handaxes that after fighting with Ug yesterday, Ig took the rest of the meat and went and hid under the big boulder?* And if not this, then what exactly? Scenarios in which a language plus module X confers more adaptive advantages than a language minus module X need to be spelled out in far greater detail if they are to carry conviction.

Perhaps under the best of circumstances such scenarios will never amount to more than just-so stories. Perhaps we are on firmer ground if we look at language as it is today and ask what evidence it affords, if any, for or against the modular nature of syntax.

For clearly, either Chomsky's hypothesized modules have neurological reality or they don't. Chomsky himself has never claimed that they have; his agnostic stance leaves it quite open as to whether the modular structure of syntactic theory in any way reflects neural realities or whether that structure represents no more than a convenient model whose effects could, in principle, be achieved by quite different kinds of neural structure. The Pinker-Bloom approach, however, suggests that we should take the modules quite literally as products of neural structures that enjoy a separate existence and that evolved at different times in the past.

Such an approach, however, raises the issue of Module-Specific Deficit (MSD). If syntax is generated by several modules, and if these modules are separately instantiated in the form of specific and distinct brain mechanisms, those mechanisms should be as subject as any other biological object to trauma and genetic defect. And if those mechanisms were affected in either way, we would expect to find MSDs in the speech of victims of some types of aphasia or dysphasia — or at least some perturbations of syntax among some definable group that would yield utterances intermediate between those of language and protolanguage.

Pinker and Bloom (1990:722) hedge this issue. First they claim one selective deficit, an impairment in the use of grammatical morphology discussed by Clahsen (1989), Gopnik (1990), and others. But on the basis of comparable cases in a morphologically rich language, Italian, Leonard et al. (1992) concluded that a perceptual rather than a grammar-specific deficit was implicated. And in any case, even in Gopnik's or Clahsen's analyses, the deficit would *not* implicate *any* of the separate syntactic modules proposed in Chomsky (1981), and therefore does not constitute an MSD in the sense of the present discussion.

However, Pinker and Bloom deny that "we should easily find cases of inherited subjacency deficiency or anaphor blindness," since "there is no reason to think that every aspect of grammar that has a genetic basis must be controlled by a single gene." I find this argument puzzling; who has ever suggested that aspects of grammar are controlled by a single gene? And anyway, what difference would it make to the possibility of MSD if they are controlled by one gene or many? Things can go wrong with parts of any complex organism if that organism contains functions that have partly or wholly distinct infrastructures. The power of the eye to focus and its sensitivity to color are two such dissociable functions, yet we find people who suffer from astigmatism or color-blindness, just as one would expect, whether a single gene or many control the underlying neural mechanisms.

Moreover, when we turn to aphasia, Pinker and Bloom's argument from genes loses its force. The regions affected by traumas to the brain are not determined by or connected with genes. Traumas can cause a wide variety of nonlinguistic deficits (see Sacks 1985 for just a few of the more bizarre of these), so why shouldn't they also cause MSDs? Even if we find no "*inherited* subjacency deficiency or anaphor blindness," why shouldn't we find similar MSDs of traumatic origin?

The strongest claim for the existence of such MSDs comes from Grodzinsky (1990; Grodzinsky et al. 1991), who describes the behavior of aphasics with respect to passives and binding. With respect to passives, Grodzinsky points out that while active sentences (e.g., *The man is pulling the kid*) were correctly interpreted by agrammatic aphasic patients at a level well above chance, their equivalent passives (e.g., *The kid is pulled by the man*) were interpreted around the chance level. Grodzinsky interpreted this differential as due to an inability to process the traces of NP-movement found in passives but not in actives.[13]

13. Generative theory accounts for passive-voice sentences in the following manner. The underlying form of a sentence such as *Bill was seen by Mary* looks something like *e was seen Bill by Mary*. Because a participle like *seen* lacks the power

There are, however, a number of problems with Grodzinsky's experiment. First is the limited number of subjects (only two in Grodzinsky 1990; four in Grodzinsky et al. 1991, selected, on grounds that remain unclear, from an original pool of eight). Then there is the experimental design, which had subjects matching pictures with sentences that the subjects assembled out of sentence fragments written on cards (for instance, to match a picture showing a child being pulled by a man, subjects were required to assemble three cards on which were, respectively, *the kid*, *the man*, and *is pulled by*). In the absence of examples of the drawings, it is hard to see how sentences such as *The man was unchallenged by the woman* or *The father was disappointed by the son* could be pictorially represented as unambiguously as *The man is untied by the woman* or *The girl is photographed by the nurse*. Thus some differentials Grodzinsky found between categories could have been a function of the subjects' puzzlement over potentially ambiguous representations.

A more serious problem is one that Grodzinsky does confront. In his original prediction, both adjectival passives (e.g., *The doctor was annoyed with the patient*) and adjectival *un*-passives (participial adjectives with a negative prefix; e.g., *The policeman was unnoticed by the criminal*) should have been interpreted equally, and equally well, since in most analyses neither type of sentence involves NP-movement. In fact, adjectival passives were well interpreted, while the equivalent *un*-passives were interpreted around the chance level (82.5 percent versus 57.5 percent correct interpretations for the two classes in Grodzinsky 1990, 79 percent versus 60 percent in Grodzinsky et al. 1991).

To account for this finding, Grodzinsky was obliged to propose a different analysis for adjectival *un*-passives, one in which they, like regular agentive passives, were produced by NP-movement, which left a trace which the subjects could not interpret. However, there is a more

---

to govern its complements that the related verb *see* possesses, *Bill* has to move to the position marked by *e* (the process known as NP-movement). However, such movement is regarded as leaving a trace (*t*) at the extraction site of the noun phrase *Bill*, so that the actual structure of the passive is *Bill was seen t by Mary*, where *t* and *Bill* are understood as coreferring with one another. Agrammatic aphasics are supposed not to be able to "see" traces and consequently cannot understand that, far from being the Agent in this sentence, *Bill* is the Theme or Patient (approximately half the time they interpret such sentences as being synonymous with *Bill saw Mary*, etc.).

parsimonious explanation, made more plausible by one of Grodzinsky's own choices: "in order to preserve the adjectival reading, adjectives with passive morphology were presented without *by*-phrases; *about-*, *with-*, *at-* and *in*-phrases were used instead" (Grodzinsky 1990:119). In other words, the difference between the levels of interpretation of adjectival passives and *un*-passives could have arisen because the second category was always accompanied by a *by*-phrase while the first category always lacked such phrases.

Suppose that agrammatics have a straightforward protolinguistic strategy that says, in effect, "The first noun-phrase in a sentence is the logical subject" (that is, Agent, or [+affected] where there is an intransitive predicate). At the same time, suppose their lexical knowledge still includes a property of the preposition *by*: "*by* always indicates Agent (or logical subject)." In active and adjectival-passive sentences the first factor alone would be present and would predict the correct result, as found; since Grodzinsky excluded *by*-phrases from the latter category, there would be no distracting effect. However, in the passive and adjectival *un*-passive sentences, a *by*-phrase was always present; agrammatics would then not know whether the first noun-phrase or the noun-phrase following *by* was the logical subject, and would give random answers, as found.

Somewhat different criticisms apply to Grodzinsky's claim that an MSD may affect the binding module (that part of the grammar which determines the reference of such words as *he, himself, each other*). The evidence presented in Grodzinsky (1990) consists simply in the fact that while (an unspecified number of) patients (whose neurological impairment is not described) interpreted the reference of reflexive pronouns correctly at a level well above chance, they showed significant differences in their interpretation of ordinary pronouns, depending on context. For instance, faced with two sentences such as *Is every bear washing her?* and *Is Mama Bear washing her?*, more subjects interpreted *her* in the second sentence as referring to *Mama Bear* than interpreted *her* as referring to *every bear* in the first (we are not told what significance level, if any, the difference between the two conditions met).

But even if we take the claim at its face value, what does it mean? According to Grodzinsky, the difference arises because quantifiers such as *every* come under a more rigorous rule than referential expressions such as *Mama* (for instance, while *his* in both *Bill loves his mother* and *His mother loves Bill* may refer to *Bill*, only *his* in *Every boy loves his mother* refers to *every boy*; in *His mother loves every boy, every boy* cannot be the antecedent of *his*). But even so, a deficit in this area is a strange candidate for an MSD. In one analysis of anaphora and coreference (Reinhardt 1983, 1986), binding theory itself is not involved; only a pragmatic rule of coreference is affected. In another (Chomsky's, cited by Grodzinsky 1990:127), Binding Principle A remains intact, and only an extension of Principle B is affected. Thus in the first interpretation the deficit is not an MSD at all, and in the second it affects only a fraction of one module.[14]

Moreover, Grodzinsky's evidence does not make clear what part(s) of syntax, if any, are spared. The fact that a subject can correctly interpret active sentences (albeit with a slightly lower success rate than normal controls) need not necessarily involve syntactic processing; a good protolinguistic strategy is to assume that the first thing an utterance refers to is probably an Agent. This is by no means to suggest that Grodzinsky's line of inquiry is in any sense unfruitful or misguided; to the contrary, far more linguists need to be looking at aphasic phenomena across a much broader range of patients. However, the jury on MSDs will have to remain out until such extended studies become available.

The absence of evidence for syntactic modules is more striking for the dysphasias. Here the evidence from Down's syndrome and other types of mental retardation (Sabsay and Kerman 1993), as well as from the study of language-deprived children (Curtiss 1977, 1988), suggests that when syntax is damaged, it is damaged in an all-or-nothing manner. Indirectly supporting this conclusion is a large and growing body of data from subjects affected by Williams' syndrome (Bellugi et al. 1991, 1994) or Prader-Willi syndrome (Burd and Kerbeshian 1989, Gardner 1994) which indicates that if mental retardation spares syntax, it spares all syntax: to date, I know of no syndrome that spares some syntactic modules while impairing others (just one such syndrome, of course, would be a striking piece of evidence in favor of a modular syntactic mechanism).

But what has all this to do with evolution? If syntax is in fact driven by the interaction of several independent modules, these can hardly have

14. Indeed, there may, as before, be a nonsyntactic explanation for the subjects' improved performance where *every* is involved. If the subject recognizes that in a phrase *every X*, despite the lack of plural marking, a plural referent is entailed, then singular *her* cannot corefer with *every bear*. Grodzinsky could check this hypothesis by seeing if his subjects do less well with *is every bear washing them?*

emerged simultaneously. The gradualist scenario in some shape or form must be correct. However, a wide range of evidence surveyed in the previous section has suggested that the evolution of syntax was more likely a single catastrophic event. If so, this predicts that there should be a single syntactic module, and a robust one at that, if it can survive along with severely impaired cognition, as the Williams' syndrome cases suggest. Nothing in the literature on the various aphasias and dysphasias seems to conflict with the hypothesis of a single syntactic module, and much supports it, as this section has shown.

The foregoing has certain implications for the neural infrastructure of language. That infrastructure must be such that if part of it is impaired, all of it is impaired. This certainly does not mean that only a single part of the brain is involved in syntax. A network linking several areas, one which cannot function unless all of its connections are in place, would fill the bill just as easily, and more plausibly. At the moment we can only speculate about what such a network might be like. Some recent work on the brain (Leiner et al. 1989, 1991; Fiez et al. 1990) implicates the neocerebellum in linguistic and other cognitive tasks; certainly this phylogenetically new area is directly linked to prefrontal language areas by both mossy and climbing fibers.[15] Intriguingly, recent research on Williams' and Down's syndrome cases (Jernigan and Bellugi 1990, Wang et al. 1992) has shown that in the former the neocerebellum is significantly larger than in the latter.

This evidence strongly suggests that if there is a single unified syntactic network, the neocerebellum forms part of that network. Given that the cerebellum functions mainly in the acceleration and automatization of behavioral routines, its involvement in syntax—which requires rapid and automatic processing—should not be unexpected. On the other hand, cerebellar lesions do not seem to be implicated in agrammatism. The answer may lie in the fact that in addition to the cerebellar differences, differences between Down's and Williams' syndrome cases involve the frontal cortex (Jernigan et al. 1993), which is normally developed in the latter but deficient in the former. Perhaps the syntactic network can survive some degree of cerebellar damage but not damage to two or more

15. The cerebellum is known to have enlarged in the hominid line almost as much as the cerebral cortex (Passingham 1975), while it contains perhaps even more cells than the cerebral cortex does (Braitenberg and Atwood 1958).

areas connected by the network. Clearly, these are empirical issues that can be resolved only by further research, in particular by a rereading of the clinical literature on agrammatism in light of recent discoveries and by the progressive improvement of techniques for brain imaging that will give us a clearer picture of what happens in the brain when sentences are produced and comprehended.

The concept of a network rather than a particular area of the brain devoted to syntax—the idea that what generates syntax is simply a single set of interconnections between areas dedicated to lexical storage, phonetic representation, the automatization of behavioral routines, and perhaps other functions—helps to account for a persistent finding in agrammatism studies: that quite severe damage to Broca's area does not necessarily entail agrammatism. Grodzinsky et al. (1991) rejected four out of the eight Broca's aphasics chosen for their study, for unspeci-fied reasons; the four they chose showed, from a clinical perspective, quite diverse patterns of impairment. If network integrity is the key to preservation of function, we would expect to find a relationship between trauma and deficit quite different from what we would find if areal in-tegrity were the crucial element. In particular, we would expect to find maintenance of function despite considerable damage if the syntactic network remained intact, and loss of function despite less severe or less widespread damage if the network was breached.

The network concept also helps to explain how the phylogenetic onset of syntax could have been sudden, with no predecessor intermediate between an asyntactic and a fully syntactical mode. The idea that a single mutation could have produced syntax (Bickerton 1990) caused more neg-ative reactions than anything else in that book. However, if all the areas involved in syntax had developed (to subserve quite different purposes, presumably) prior to the onset of syntax, if no dedicated network of connections linked them at this stage, and if such a network constituted a necessary and sufficient precondition for syntax, it should be obvious that a single mutation could do the trick.

A network is not a network until it is complete. Imagine a newly con-structed factory lying idle because someone neglected to make a crucial connection in the electric wiring. The making of that single connection is all that is needed to turn a dark and silent edifice into a pulsing, brilliantly lit workplace. This could have been how syntax evolved in the brain. Immediately prior to true language, all but the final connection may have been present, yet it would have been as if the network did not exist. Then the final linkage was made, and suddenly a machine of tremendous power was up and running.

However, that machine was constituted, it turned the human brain into an inference engine powerful enough to make possible the totally unprecedented cultural explosion of the last fifty millennia. More remarkable still, it achieved this without adding a single cubic centimeter to a brain that had been growing steadily for two million years without producing the minutest fraction of what it subsequently produced. What that machine made possible in terms of thought and consciousness forms the topic of the remainder of this book.

Chapter 3

Language and intelligence

To many people, what most clearly distinguishes our species from others is our superior intelligence, rather than language. Some problems with this viewpoint were suggested in the previous chapter. Intelligence is often equated with brain size, but as we saw, brain sizes within the modern human range were first attained over a million years ago, at least a million years before traces of seriously enhanced intelligence showed up in the fossil record. I therefore argued that only some reorganization of existing brain structure could have caused the explosion of human culture that began a few tens of thousands of years ago and that (for better or worse) is far from over. I argued too that all that this reorganization did was convert a stumbling, halting protolanguage into the superb and infinitely flexible instrument that all of us control today.

Of course you could accept the first part of the argument without accepting the second. Maybe there was some great brain reorganization a few tens of thousands of years ago, but it had nothing to do with language per se. It simply made us more intelligent, and only then were we able to invent language as we now know it. This sounds plausible, if a little vague. In fact it sounds plausible *because* it is vague. If you try to make it more precise, it begins to look much more problematic.

Why a simple "growth-of-intelligence" model won't work

One problem with intelligence is that it constitutes no genuine category. It covers a whole range of capacities. If you want to test for astigmatism or sobriety or HIV or diphtheria, a single test does the trick for each. But any intelligence test consists of word meanings, basic arithmetic, basic logic, the capacity to form analogies, the capacity to mentally rotate figures, and on and on. Yet not one of these capacities, in isolation, would be taken as proof of intelligence. To the contrary, someone may have one capacity—say, the ability to perform mathematical calculations—enhanced far beyond an average person's, but lacking other capacities may be regarded as mentally subnormal (the well-known savant syndrome, see Sacks 1985). It is the cooperative interaction of these capacities that leads us to assume the presence of intelligence.

The more faculties our intelligence involves, the less likely it is that this intelligence could have come into existence as suddenly as the fossil record indicates. No evolutionary change emerges out of the blue, nor does such a change affect several different faculties simultaneously. Thus it is unlikely that most or all the faculties of which intelligence is composed should have undergone radical change at exactly the same time. One of them, maybe—even two is stretching things a bit. It's much more likely that some single new faculty emerged, one that of its very nature was able to transform a whole range of preexisting faculties.

Let's begin by rethinking what intelligence really is, and, perhaps still more important, what it is for. The belief that intelligence is (or at least is evidenced by) the ability to solve problems has led some theorists in artificial intelligence to compare human brains to computers, and even to suggest that some distinctive features of human minds, such as consciousness, may eventually arise in computers. This belief forms part of a syndrome that should be known as Computer-Assisted Pygmalionism, or the CAP syndrome. I'll return to this in the next chapter. For now I'd like to point out one radical difference in problem solving between animals and machines.

The problems animals solve, the problems we solve, are our *own* problems. Typically they are problems like, how can I get to eat, how can I avoid some life-threatening danger, how can I mate and breed. For us, *Homo sapiens sapiens*, sometimes those problems are a little more complex and a little less pressing, such as determining which U.S. city provides the best quality of life, or how black can mate in three. But the problems computers solve are not problems for computers. If I have a problem, it's my problem. If my computer has a problem, it's still my problem. Nothing is a problem for it, because it doesn't interact with the world. It just sits there and waits for me to give it *my* problems.

One should not, of course, confuse a computer with a robot. Both are mechanical creatures that carry out rational processes of computation; one may encounter some of the physical consequences of those computations, the other almost certainly will not, but this may appear as the only significant difference. However, by virtue of acting in the real world, the robot commits itself to a type of existence similar to that which animals enjoy. Although its actual resources may be heavily determined by the current state of the art, those resources are not restricted *in principle*; a robot could in principle seek nourishment, avoid danger, and perhaps even mate with other robots. In such a case, robots would come under exactly the same kinds of selective pressures as living creatures. Whether they could respond adaptively is, of course, a separate issue.

Let us consider intelligence in evolutionary terms; hopefully it will soon be regarded as irresponsible to think about mind and intelligence in any other terms. We will thus stop thinking about intelligence as problem solving and begin to look at it as a way of maintaining homeostasis. Homeostasis means simply the preservation of those conditions that are most favorable to an organism, the optimal achievable conditions for its survival and well-being. If intelligence had not served to maintain homeostasis, it would never have come into existence, for intelligence requires a brain, and brains are complex and use lots of energy—maybe as much as 20 percent of one's total energy budget.

Increasing the complexity of the brain does not, of course, represent the only, or even the most popular, way of achieving homeostasis. As the proverb has it, "The fox knows many things, but the hedgehog knows one big thing." The one big thing the hedgehog (a kind of European porcupine) knows is to roll itself into a ball with its spines extended: this suffices to save it in most situations. Understandably, far more creatures have gone the hedgehog route than have gone the fox route: it is more energy-conserving and requires less complex apparatus. The high energy costs of even modest brain increments put them beyond the price range of all but a small animal elite. The vast majority rely on some master device like spines in the case of the hedgehog, protective coloration in the case of many insects, release of pungent chemicals in the case of the skunk, and so on. Why go to the length of developing a costly and cumbersome brain if One Good Trick can do the job? Equipped with such a device, a species can survive indefinitely.

But at least some species will take the brain route. There is what is re-ferred to as an "escalation" (Vermeij 1987) or "arms races" (Dawkins and Krebs 1979, Van Valen 1973), in which some improvement in a predator's skills selects for improvement in those of a prey species, and vice versa. Of course, not all these skills involve brain improvements, but some will; analysis by Jerison (1973) has shown that, over evolutionary time, brain sizes of prey and predator species have gradually increased in tandem (with predators ever so slightly in the lead). There is the autocatalytic behavioral accelerator first noted by Allan Wilson (1991) by which novel behaviors that prove advantageous select for brain improvements that facilitate those behaviors: the greater a creature's plasticity and the wider the range of its behaviors, the more frequently both habits and brain improvements will occur. All forms of brain improvement tend to be preserved (so that they become the foundation for further improvements) by a kind of ratchet effect: for creatures living in high-energy zones, loss of computational power within an ecology of intact competitors spells speedy death for the individual and extinction for the species.

Is there a *scala naturae* of intelligence?

Over the course of evolution, the highest level of intelligence found at any given time among creatures in general has tended to increase—not to give one species an advantage over another, but simply to maintain species at the same level of adaptive fitness, of homeostasis. But how, and how much, and by what stages has intelligence increased? If we look naïvely at the broad range of creatures, we tend to come up with intuitive judgments. We feel that a frog exceeds an amoeba in intelligence, a dog exceeds a frog, a chimp exceeds a dog, and we, it goes without saying, exceed a chimp. Is this scientifically valid, or just another piece of folk psychology?

Earlier this century, hardcore behaviorists said yes, that's just folk psychology. The brain begins as a tabula rasa. Intelligence results from learning. Learning results from responses to stimuli that get reinforced. Anything can learn anything if you give the right stimulus and encourage the right response to that stimulus.

Later, people found that these things were not so. No brain is a tabula rasa. Lots of things that seem like intelligent behavior are hardwired in. Animals differ widely in what they can learn, no matter how often you give stimuli and reward responses. The idea spread that intelligence was niche specific. An animal adapted to a niche, and developed a specialized intelligence to deal with the problems peculiar to that niche. Forms of intelligence might differ wildly and unpredictably from one species to another.

In the early 1980s, the British psychologist Euan McPhail (1982, 1987) made a very different proposal. According to McPhail, nature knows only three levels of intelligence. The first level consists of animals able to forge links between stimuli and responses, in other words of S-R (stimulus-response) animals. Practically all creatures are S-R animals. The second level consists of animals that can link a stimulus with another stimulus, in other words S-S (stimulus-stimulus) animals. All vertebrates, and many invertebrates, are S-S animals. As for the third level, we'll come to that in a moment.

What the second level of intelligence did was what the poet Paul Valery, cited by François Jacob (1982), re-cited by philosopher Daniel Dennett (1991), called "producing future." S-R animals cannot produce future: they can react only when something directly affects them. S-S animals can produce a little future, like Pavlov's dogs who knew that when a bell rang, food was coming. The ability to produce future can make the difference between life and death: that's why there are so many S-S animals today.

If there are really only these two levels of intelligence, what does the folk-psychology picture of a wide range of intelligence levels derive from, and why does it seem so widespread, so deep-rooted, and so intuitively satisfying? There are several reasons. One is the distinction between creatures that can learn and those dominated by what used to be called "instinct." This is not really a distinction but a graded continuum: all creatures, including ourselves, have some fixed action patterns, while even protozoa can habituate, a primitive kind of learning (Applewhite 1973). But because the continuum is graded, and because we are at the learning end, we perceive intelligence as a continuum and assume that learned behaviors need more intelligence than hardwired ones.

Something that also determines our impressions of intelligence is the range of behaviors that a particular species exhibits. Amoeba don't have very many, dogs have more than frogs, and so on. Frogs can't play fetch because they can't do goal-directed running or carry things in their mouths, because they don't process their visual input enough to recognize you, and because object retrieval plays no part in their froggy existence. None of this provides any reasoned basis for assuming differences in reasoning powers between the two creatures. Yet, other things being equal, creatures with more behaviors, like dogs, will seem to us smarter than those with fewer, like frogs.

Another factor that influences our assessment is a creature's degree of similarity to ourselves. How much of the intelligence we attribute to chimps results from the way chimps are built, as compared to, say, dogs? Dogs cannot manipulate things; we and chimps can. Dogs cannot sit up and use their paws at tea tables or in kiddy cars; we and chimps can.

This may not explain all the apparent differences in intelligence between chimps and dogs, but it surely accounts for a lot of them.

So it could be that apparent differences in intelligence arise from a combination of these three factors—our bias in favor of learning, our overvaluation of broad behavioral ranges, and our fondness for creatures like ourselves—as well as, perhaps, others. Certainly, since McPhail laid down his challenge, nobody has produced evidence to refute him. But what about McPhail's third level? That, according to McPhail, was provided by language. In 1987, neither he nor any of the thirty-odd psychologists and others who wrote commentaries on McPhail (1987)—myself included—had a very clear idea how language enhanced intelligence. But I think I am at last beginning to get a handle on it.

On-line versus off-line thinking

That handle depends on the oft-neglected but basic and crucial distinction between on-line and off-line thinking made in the previous chapter. Recall that on-line thinking involves computations carried out only in terms of neural responses elicited by the presence of external objects, while off-line thinking involves computations carried out on more lasting internal representations of those objects. Such computations need not be initiated by external causes, nor need they initiate an immediate motor response. What differentiates human from nonhuman thought, and what has led many, like Gazzaniga (1985:163), to deny thinking to other species, is that while all creatures above a pretty low level of brain organization can practice on-line thinking (to widely varying extents, I need hardly add), only humans can practice both on-line and off-line thinking.

Now if the prime function of intelligence is to maintain homeostasis in creatures, it follows that the original role for intelligence was to perform on-line thinking. It is now, not in some hypothetical future, still less in some irrecoverable past, that creatures have to save themselves from predators, find food and water, seek mates, and sow their progeny. From an evolutionary perspective, on-line thinking achieves all that a creature needs.

Of course, on-line thinking does not achieve all that a creature might want, if it could want. It would obviously be beneficial to individuals if they could predict where a predator would be likeliest to lie in wait, and then avoid that place. It would be beneficial to an entire species to be able to figure out some means of trapping and killing its major predators, and apply that means until predators were wiped out or at least drastically reduced in numbers. But such luxury homeostatic options, available to and frequently exercised by our own species, are not available to others.

Yet the fact that on-line thinking works as well as it does to preserve the lives and well-being of creatures means that there could have been no selective pressure for off-line thinking to develop. This in turn makes it unlikely that off-line thinking developed directly out of on-line thinking. In the previous chapter it was shown that a mildly continuist scenario— one in which a small initial brain expansion yielded more neurons than were needed for on-line thinking—could explain how meaningful utterances first got understood. However, that scenario includes one grave disadvantage that outweighs any advantages it might have.

In on-line thinking, the ingredients of the problem (whether it is a problem set by nature or one set by humans under laboratory conditions) are all present, even the complex problems set for chimpanzees nearly three-quarters of a century ago by Kohler (1927) or the more recent experiments carried out by Premack (1983). Some solutions in both cases showed high degrees of skill, a skill Premack felt obliged to account for by hypothesizing the existence, among primates, of an abstract code intermediate between the "imaginal code" with which most creatures operate and language. This code Premack tried to characterize in terms of "tags" attached to concepts such as (varying kinds or degrees of) shape, size, color, purpose and so on: a number of commentators on Premack's paper (Bickerton 1983b, Haber 1983, Marschak 1983, Millward 1983) expressed considerable skepticism about the status, infrastructure, and evolutionary provenance of such tags.

But one point was perhaps not made clearly enough by any of those commentators. This point involves a curious discrepancy between what Premack was claiming and what his experimental results actually showed. The data Premack had to account for distinguished between performances of untrained chimpanzees on the one hand, and young children and "language"-trained chimpanzees on the other. It did not demonstrate any differences between untrained chimpanzees and members of other primate (or nonprimate) species. In other words, it distinguished between subjects that had been exposed to language or some kind of quasi-linguistic symbolic system and subjects that had not, and it did nothing more than that. If all that distinguished these groups was some degree of language exposure, one would conclude that there is no intermediate system between what Premack calls the imaginal code—that is, whatever medium is used by alingual creatures to do their on-line thinking—and some form of language or protolanguage, accessible to children and trained apes alike.

Premack (1983:132) dismisses this possibility on the grounds that language "does not instil the [abstract] code—as probably no training could—but if the species has the code to start with, the training enhances the animal's ability to use it." Granted that no training could instil any code for which the infrastructure was not present, it doesn't follow that chimpanzees possess a code systematically distinguishing them from nonprimates (or nonpongids) on the one hand, and humans on the other. A more parsimonious explanation, although one that Premack failed to consider, is that the imaginal code itself—the system of categories into which creatures must sort experience, or the PRS, in terms of Bickerton (1990)—constitutes, in sufficiently developed species, an infrastructure fully adequate for subsequent acquisition of a protolanguage-like "linguistic code."

How could this be? Suppose an animal has well-developed concepts but they are not filed as single units under category-specific labels. Rather they are distributed across the processing areas devoted to the various senses. Nowhere is there "just cat": there is an auditory cat, a visual cat, an olfactory cat, and so on. This works fine, since any of these distributed cat representations will, under appropriate stimulation, enable the animal to recognize the presence of a cat. Likewise, under appropriate circumstances, any of those same distributed representations will fire the motor sequences that give appropriate behavioral responses to manifestations of cat. Yet even though these representations may be cross-modally linked, there is no convergence zone in which all their attributes are summarized, so to speak. Teach the animal a word or sign for cat, and you automatically create that place: a space in the brain where for the first time there is represented something that stands for the whole cat and nothing but the cat. Whether or not this account is correct, in contrast with Premack's it places the behavioral Rubicon where it actually lies: between untrained animals (primates and nonprimates alike) on the one hand and "language"-trained animals and humans on the other. Moreover, Premack's hypothesis of some specialized code peculiar

Figure 3.1

The protolanguage family tree

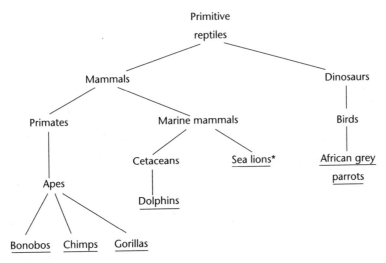

*Underlined animals are those that have been shown experimentally to possess protolinguistic ability

to primates fails to explain the acquisition of protolanguage by species which, as Figure 3.1 shows, are phylogenetically far removed from the primate line.[1]

If there is no evidence for any significant behavioral Rubicon either between chimpanzees and other apes or between primates and other species (but a great deal of commonality among a variety of species when it comes to picking up protolinguistic skills), we should be suspicious of any undocumented and empirically unmotivated system intermediate between the two representational systems addressed in Bickerton (1990):

1. Whether the degree of acquisition differs as between different species is an interesting though not particularly relevant question. No researcher has conclusively demonstrated any significant difference between the capacities of dolphins, sea lions, parrots, or apes in this respect, and this in turn tends to support the claim that no "intermediate," quasi-symbolic system needs to be invoked in order to account for the empirical evidence. For if primates had such an intermediate code, it should enable them, when exposed to protolanguage, to acquire greater proficiency than species lacking that code.

the primary system based on sensory input and the secondary system based on language.[2] All the activities described by Kohler, Premack, and others who have experimented with the cognitive capacities of apes were on-line operations. There do not seem to have been any experiments requiring a delay between the posing of a problem and its solution, or any other circumstance that would suggest, if the experiment were successful, that the subject must have carried out any form of off-line computation. Until such experiments are carried out, or until adequate anecdotal evidence emerges from ethological studies, parsimony suggests that we refrain from hypothesizing either off-line thinking in other creatures or mysterious codes or capacities intermediate between direct sensory representation and (some form of) language.[3]

Writers like Premack (1983) and Donald (1991) err in supposing that for cognitive development to reach the human level some kind of third, intermediate stage was required between the sensory representations of McPhail's S-R animals and the linguistic representations of humans. The opposite error is made by Jackendoff (1987:31), who sees a "similar transition" between simple and complex living organisms as is found between simple (e.g., a thermostat) and complex (e.g., a computer) machines. It is uninteresting to talk about the computational capacities of thermostats or paramecia (the latter are better described in biological or chemical terms), but past a certain level (Jackendoff suggests that of "insects or spiders or squids"—roughly the level at which McPhail's S-R animals begin) computational capacities become nontrivial.

That there might be a discontinuity anywhere in this Grand Chain of Computational Being—a discontinuity such as the emergence of the ca-

2. This argument applies equally to the "mimetic" intermediate stage suggested by Davidson and Noble (1989) and hypothesized by Donald (1991). Insofar as mimesis is understood as something more than mere imitation (aping!), it involves holding steady and unchanged some kind of representation of whatever is being interpreted mimetically. It seems reasonable to suppose that such representations are a function of (some kind of) language and that accordingly it is unsurprising that no species other than ours is capable of mimesis in Donald's sense. The attention the idea has received is surprising, considering that it violates parsimony and is empirically unsupported.

3. William Calvin (personal communication) has pointed out that such experiments (as well as being hard to design) would be of their nature irreplicable, since they would involve open-ended and unpredictable outcomes. They would not, however, for that reason be lacking in interest.

pacity for off-line as well as on-line computation — is nowhere suggested by Jackendoff, so it is pointless to speculate what he might say about such a proposal. This is a pity, as his theory of mind and consciousness is more thoroughly developed than most, and I shall accordingly return to it in this and the next chapter.

How off-line thinking molds human behavior

Let's start by looking at some typical aspects of off-line thinking as it manifests itself in behavior. Though we may think we can look into our own brains, we cannot look into the brains of dogs and chimps, so only on the basis of behavior do we form impressions of other animals' intelligence. It seems reasonable, therefore, to use the same criteria on ourselves.

Suppose you were an alien from another planet, and the first human you saw was engaged in punching a leather ball on the end of a long spring. You might imagine that the man was angry with the ball. Or perhaps you might guess that the man was angry at someone or something else, and had simply displaced his anger upon an object that was unable to fight back. And then suppose that the second human you saw was posturing in front of a large mirror, and performing a variety of movements with her arms and legs. You might assume that the woman was excessively vain, and derived gratification from admiring her own suppleness and skill. In both cases, of course, you would be quite wrong.

Neither the boxer nor the dancer is engaged in activities that yield immediate satisfaction. They may even be tiresome chores. The boxer is training for a forthcoming fight; the dancer is rehearsing for a performance. Look at how alien these behaviors are to any species but our own. Try to imagine a tiger practicing its killing technique in the absence of any prey, or a gazelle practicing its latest escape maneuver in the absence of any predator.

You may say, animals do practice their various behaviors when young: their play as cubs is vital for acquiring skills they will need later in life. But this confuses two very different things. After all, human infants play like any other young animals, and acquire basic skills in doing so. But adult humans can do something extra. Quite deliberately, in later life, they can train themselves in particular forms of behavior. Moreover, cubs train for only the things that all cubs do. Humans train for highly specialized things that most humans don't do. Few of us become boxers or dancers, although we may become surfers or golfers or distance runners or any of a million other things. Doing a special, individualized thing simply to be able to do it better on some future occasion is uniquely human behavior.

It is also behavior that would be impossible without off-line thinking. In order to engage in such behavior, we have first to select (perhaps unconsciously, or for motives that may remain unclear to us) what it is that we want to do. We then have to study that behavior, to take it to pieces (or allow some instructor to do this for us) and practice its parts both in isolation (the dancer performing repeatedly a new step she has just learned) and in combination (the boxer going a couple of rounds with his sparring partner). Driving this whole procedure is a vision of how a great boxer or great dancer should behave, based perhaps on an ideal amalgam of the traits of great boxers and dancers of the past. All of this activity (forming an ideal, breaking it down, reassembling it) involves mentally representing behaviors none of which we need necessarily perform at the time of representation and some of which we may never achieve no matter how much energy we may devote to the attempt.

Premack (1985) saw pedagogy, rather than language, as the major distinguishing feature of our species: no other species deliberately sets out to impart knowledge or skills to fellow species members, although of course other creatures can and do learn from observing one another.[4] But whether human learning occurs through pedagogy or is autodidactic, the processes entail that a potentially infinite number of actions and relations between actions be mentally represented in the physical absence of those actions. What is claimed here is not that such things are mentally represented in language, but that they are represented in the neural workspace that was originally created by and for language. In

---

4. However, see Boesch (1993) for a striking demonstration of pedagogy in Ivory Coast chimpanzees. This makes Premack's claim look dubious, but does it constitute a counterexample to what is argued here? No, because Boesch's chimps were *simply doing what they were teaching* (that is, they were simply opening nuts, and engaged neither in devising better techniques for opening nuts nor in breaking down the process of nut-opening into components that could be studied separately). But a trainer instructing a boxer (even if he does so wordlessly) is not boxing, and a teacher instructing a dancer (even if she merely demonstrates the steps) is not dancing. In other words, wholly different analyses of what is taught and learned are available to humans.

other words, if we had not acquired language we would not be able to represent such things.

The capacity to represent ideal (or at least, superior) performance is what enables us to perform mental or physical rehearsals for future actions. This in turn makes possible what in Bickerton (1990) was called "constructional learning." Those who can learn only from experience or observation are at the mercy of happenstance. But those who can practice constructional learning, who can analyze memories of past events and use the product of that analysis to affect future events, will be able to avoid pitfalls that others cannot. However, such things can be done only if thinking is detached from the thinker's immediate environment, encapsulated from immediate interaction with the world, and carried out with the "just-a-cat, just-a-mat" kind of representations created for language and stripped of all their irrelevant particularities.

Let's look more closely at this characteristic of detachment, since one of the features of off-line thinking is that it can occur simultaneously with on-line thinking. Imagine you are driving to work and thinking about a committee meeting that awaits you there. You foresee problems. You believe your position is correct but you know you'll be facing strong opposition. Deep in your mental rehearsal of how to defend yourself and how you may be attacked and how you can respond to those attacks, you are scarcely aware of the traffic flow around you or your hands and feet controlling the car. Then a ball bounces in front of you and the meeting scenario vanishes, replaced at the heart of your awareness by a vivid street scene, which, as you brake, you scan furiously for the small child you expect will follow the bouncing ball. None does, and you accelerate and are back at the meeting, running on automatic again.

Both driving and mental rehearsal constitute intelligent behaviors. At least they are behaviors for which we have not yet succeeded in deputizing members of other species, or even robots of our own construction. At first they may seem to differ strikingly. The first, an example of on-line thinking, involves interaction with the outside world; the second, typical of off-line thinking, takes place wholly within your own mind, wherever or whatever that may turn out to be. Yet what you are responding to, in both types of activity, is simply an excitation of neurons in different parts of the brain. One activity draws on immediate sensory input, the other does not; but qua thought, qua computational process, it's not clear how one would distinguish between them—unless the processes in fact take place in quite distinct areas of the brain, one hooked to motor output (so that you no sooner see the bouncing ball than you brake) and one not (so that you do not, unless you are emotionally disturbed, pound the wheel of the car with your fist whenever you think of the committee chairman's intransigence).

Some of us might want to say that the second activity is somehow higher—more mindful, hence more important and more truly human than the first. If asked why, we might say something like, "Well, driving behavior is, or at least can be, quite unconscious—you may drive for many minutes involved in some thought or other, not paying the slightest attention to where you are going, and then suddenly realize you have not the faintest conception of the route you followed in order to get to where you now are."[5] Conversely, we might say, meeting-rehearsal behavior must always be conscious. You can hardly prepare for a meeting without being fully aware that you are preparing for a meeting. Now a behavior that is conscious provides us with the feeling that we control that behavior (whether that feeling has any foundation in fact is quite another matter). At least we have some degree of introspective access to it. In contrast, we have no access to the mechanisms that control on-line thinking. Because we are prejudiced in favor of things we can introspect and think we can control, a behavior that is not conscious is automatically downgraded to the level of automatic behavior, and correspondingly disrespected.

But the conscious-unconscious dichotomy does not fit the facts quite so neatly. Take our supposedly necessary consciousness of the meeting rehearsal. When the ball bounced into the roadway, your consciousness of that previous activity temporarily disappeared. Did it disappear because the activity ceased, or was it merely that your attention was switched away from it? There's some good anecdotal evidence suggesting that just such "higher," "conscious" processes may go on quite without our awareness—stories of scientists and mathematicians who had abandoned problems as insoluble only to come up with the answer while engaged in some totally irrelevant activity (Hadamard 1945). So

5. Dennett (1991:137) regards this phenomenon as "rolling consciousness with swift memory loss": something which would seem, of its very nature, unconfirmable. In the two-level theory of consciousness elaborated in the following chapter, there is no need to hypothesize untestable conditions. See the section entitled "Some Puzzles of Consciousness."

it would seem that "higher mental activity" can continue in the absence of conscious awareness.

What about the other, supposedly lower kind of thinking, the on-line kind? That, as we have seen, may be largely or completely unconscious, only to leap into the glare of consciousness when some feature of the environment or some event comes into our purview and demands our immediate and conscious attention. We are left, not with higher or lower, conscious or unconscious forms of thinking, but with processes that differ from one another only in that one kind necessarily influences and is influenced by external factors while the other does not necessarily either cause or undergo external influence.

Human and animal thought

If mental rehearsal is to be done in time for a committee meeting, now only minutes away, it won't do to let unconscious processes take their own sweet time. Such a rehearsal must be consciousness driven, and for a mental process to be consciousness driven the focus of attention has to be withdrawn from whatever your body is currently doing and applied exclusively to that process. In evolutionary terms, this was a high risk, high gain strategy. High risk, because however smart you were, you might be deep in thought and a sabertooth tiger could jump you and none of your brilliant genes would pass to the next generation. High gain, because by means of constructional learning you could eventually arrive, as we have, at a state where at least some of us don't need to worry about where our next meal is coming from nor have to watch out for predators other than those of our own kind.

Although there is nothing to stop us attributing to other creatures all manner of thought processes similar to ours, there is no evidence for their existence and some good evolutionary reasons why they should not exist. First is the risk element already mentioned: to withdraw attention from the immediate environment can drastically shorten your life. Second, it is no use detaching yourself from your environment if you have no way of representing things except to invoke immediate behavioral consequences. Neither reason is, of course, conclusive. A third is more powerful.

We have now observed many members of many other species quite carefully over long periods, yet no one has reported any behavior that would oblige us to attribute humanlike thinking processes—off-line thinking—to them. But the capacity to think humanly must lead to changes in behavior, some of which (if our own case is anything to go by) should be fairly obvious. Moreover, the power this capacity gives, the power to think about things while delaying or suppressing immediate reactions to those things, can generate much more radical and effective action if and when the time becomes ripe for it. All other creatures adapt to environments slowly, by genetic change; our species adapts to environments rapidly, by cultural change. For that matter, we can adapt the environment to suit ourselves, as we do with snowplows, de-icing equipment, air conditioning, irrigation, and countless other inventions. The ability to adapt the environment to oneself guarantees evolutionary success in the short run (what it guarantees in the long run may be very different, since we can't control or even predict all the effects unleashed by our "improvements"). But it guarantees success precisely because it makes available a series of changes in the species that possesses it—changes that, if they occurred, could hardly hope to escape detection.

It is not a matter of choice whether a creature with this ability to change should conceal or reveal the ability. It is a matter of evolutionary necessity—inevitability, in fact. The mechanisms are simple. Any animal with even a fraction of human thinking capacity could adapt more quickly to its environment or could in some way, however, slight, tailor the environment to suit its requirements better. Any animals that could do this would live longer and have more offspring than those that could not. Their offspring would carry the same traits and there would soon be lots of these animals changing rapidly, changing themselves to fit the environment or the environment to fit themselves. We would see them doing it, even if they had no language to tell us what they were doing. But we see no such animals, not even among our immediate ancestors or closest relatives. We see ourselves, who happen to have these capacities and who happen—quite coincidentally, many will assure us—to have language.

But language is the only thing that could have provided us with the means to free our thoughts from the exigencies of the moment and to structure them into complex wholes. I can't repeat often enough that language is something added to what other creatures have in the way of intelligence. It doesn't take over the whole domain of thought. Humans like other creatures interact with their environment, and like other creatures they process the data from their sense organs to create a primary representation of the world. There's nothing mysterious about this. Except in the simplest of creatures, messages do not go directly from sense organ to motor cell. They go to processing units where they compete with other messages and the strongest message then activates motor cells. If the sensory image is of a particular kind of predator, a particular set of neurons activates. If the image is of a potential mate or a food substance, other sets will fire. The sum of all the sets fired by external objects or events (all the things and events which a given creature can recognize and distinguish between) makes up a creature's primary representation of the world, just as the sum of all responses to these firings makes up a creature's behavior.

It seems reasonable to use the term *thought* for processes that take place within the domain of primary representation. They are, after all, computational processes. A bat using its sonar to track down and capture a moth that is taking violent evasive action is carrying out such a process. Unconscious thinking, you may say. Surely, but so was Poincaré's discovery of Fuchsian functions. If you deny the title to the one, you must deny it to the other.

What's important about bat thought is that it focuses on the immediate environment only: on-line thinking cannot spill over into the past or the future or the remote in space. The process begins when the bat first locks on to the moth — that is, with the excitation of those cells in a bat's brain whose firing rate changes on receiving the sonar image of a moth in flight. It ends when the bat loses the moth or eats it, thereby causing those cells' firing rate to return to its unexcited norm. We have no reason to assume that the bat continues to think about moths, comparing the taste of this one to the taste of the last one it caught, or thinking how it might improve its success rate for moth catching, as humans might do if they caught and ate moths.

Human thought is not limited in this way, precisely because humans have a level of secondary representation. On this level, what is represented at the primary level is repeated in ways that are more tightly organized but also more abstract. If our ancestors' brains contained clusters of neurons that responded to the sight or smell or sound of a sabertooth tiger, there would have developed, at the dawn of protolanguage, an additional cluster that responded to the thought of, or word for, a sabertooth tiger. If there was just the primary representation, there would be no way to think of sabertooth tigers without immediately performing some defensive or evasive action that constituted an appropriate response to a sabertooth tiger.

Origins of human thinking

As noted in the last chapter, the claim that at least two separate levels of representation exist among humans has been confirmed by neurological studies. And we have seen that the setting up of a second kind of area was a procedure that had to occur if language, or even protolanguage, was ever to come into existence. But if all it takes to do off-line thinking is to have two kinds of brain area, one directly connected to motor functions, the other not, why shouldn't evolution have produced the second kind of area in creatures without language? Given the benefits that accrue from off-line thinking, one might claim that evolution should select for it.

The question is natural but misses the need to have two things simultaneously in operation. An area in which to represent things is useless without a means by which you can represent them: some kind of symbolic code.

But if all representation consists at bottom of electrochemical activity in the brain, why isn't such activity, given its own brain area detached from motor activities, sufficient to support off-line thinking? It is, of course; but how would the brain open up not just a new file, but a new *kind* of file, one in which activity did *not* have to be triggered (as it was in all other files) by external input, but could be triggered by internal input *alone*?

In "external input" I include proprioceptive input and input from other autonomic systems, such as the one that regulates biological fluid levels. An animal, informed by the latter mechanism that it was thirsty, and by memory of the location of a waterhole, would head for that waterhole without further stimulus. But for off-line thinking to occur, we would need the memory of the waterhole alone (in the absence of thirst, leopards, or any other external input) to trigger the memory of the animal's last visit there, the memory of a leopard lurking near there, and a consequent resolve that whenever it *did* feel thirsty it would avoid that waterhole if at all possible. How do you get one concept to trigger another in the absence of external input, when everything is hooked up (for good homeostatic, evolutionary reasons) so as to respond to external input?

The issue of what initiates cell activity is crucial in understanding the origins of off-line thinking. For off-line thinking to take place, one set of cells in the brain, without any necessary stimulus from either the environment or the creature's own autonomic systems, has to stimulate another set, and the second set a third, and so on. Moreover, every one of the many sets involved in the simplest act of off-line thinking must fulfill the same two conditions: not only must they all be able to fire without external *input*, they must also be able to fire without external *output* in the form of motor activity.

To achieve these ends, the new sets of cells must constitute some kind of representation that differs in kind from those of the primary representational system, which of their very nature are triggered by external input and precipitate external output. The new representations must fulfill the role of Perseus's mirror, which allowed the hero to confront the Gorgon indirectly, without being turned into stone, and vanquish it. In other words, they can only be bleached and denatured kinds of representation ("just a cat," "just a mat")—strong enough to evoke the properties of what they represent, yet not strong enough to provoke the reactions appropriate to what they represent. The only obvious candidates for such a level of representation are those that underlie the symbols of language, whether those symbols be words or manual signs.

The conclusion toward which this line of reasoning drives us is that protolanguage preceded off-line thinking, perhaps even by a longish margin. Only after protolanguage had created a reasonably large stock of linguistic concepts could these concepts be utilized to initiate off-line thinking[6]—in other words, only after some kind of critical mass had been attained. (Obviously if one has only a couple of dozen symbolic units, there is not much one can either think or say.) Thus if (as suggested in Bickerton 1990) the *habilis-erectus* boundary marks the very first emergence of protolanguage, we would not expect to see the taming of fire, the

---

6. By a linguistic concept I mean here nothing more than the set of cells in an area free of obligatory-input and obligatory-output connections, the synchronous firing of which could, but need not necessarily, fire synchronously the set of motor cells that would initiate pronunciation of whatever word represented the linguistic concept in question. In other words, it is misleading to equate "linguistic concept" with "representation of a word." Strictly speaking, there is no representation of words, period. There is representation of a linguistic concept (that is, a holistic concept, subsuming all of the various sensory concepts) and there is representation of a particular phonemic or orthographic form that is linked to that concept. "Word" is simply an emergent property that appears whenever a linguistic concept is linked with a corresponding phonemic or orthographic representation.

use of shelters, and the Eurasian diaspora of *erectus*—behavioral changes that presumably arose from the degree of environmental mastery that protolanguage conferred—occurring at the very beginning of *erectus*'s lifetime. Indeed, hundreds of millennia seem to have elapsed before such changes did occur.

Moreover, we can now account for a paradox noted, but not explained, in Bickerton (1990): although protolanguage derives from prior systems of representation rather than from prior systems of communication, and functions primarily as a representational system, it could have been brought into existence only through communicative use. Protolanguage, although essentially representational, could not have contributed to thinking processes until such a critical mass had been achieved. Thus even though an enhanced representational capacity was what would eventually transform hominids into humans, that capacity cannot have been what was being selected for in the dawn of protolanguage.

It is not unusual, in evolution, for a trait to be originally adaptive for one purpose and then continue to be adaptive for a different or some-times an additional purpose. Thus swim bladders have become lungs and cooling devices have become wings; but the lungs of lungfish still helped to maintain their buoyancy, and the wings of flying insects still helped to lower their body temperature. In a similar way, protolanguage—before it grew large enough to affect thinking—would have been selected for purely on the basis of its communicative function. A language not large enough to think in is large enough to warn in, or to exchange vital information about current food sources. Such things brought immediate adaptive benefits, and conferred a selective advantage on those individ-uals who became skilled in forming and interpreting the earliest stages of protolanguage.

There is also a more general argument for supposing that protolan-guage produced thought, rather than vice versa. It is an argument from parsimony. Protolanguage had to lead to the creation of cells whose patterns of connections preadapted them for off-line thinking, because by its very nature protolanguage requires such cells: if you cannot use words without an external stimulus and an immediate motor effect, what you have is not a protolanguage but a call system. Thus creation of any form of language ultimately entails off-line thinking.

If, however (contrary to what is proposed here), off-line thinking came first and formed a preadaptation for protolanguage, either off-line thinking was bootstrapped into existence by something else or it was not. The possibility that it was germinated direct is rendered unlikely by the "critical mass" considerations discussed above. Since creatures in general seem to be limited to one focus of attention at a time (see the discussion of attention mechanisms in Chapter 4), that focus cannot be fixed simultaneously on both off-line and on-line processes. If it is fixed on off-line processes, on-line processes must be ignored (at least temporarily). But on-line processes are a creature's defense against its enemies: a moment's relaxation of vigilance may prove fatal. So, off-line thinking must provide substantial benefits that will offset such potential losses. But off-line thinking cannot provide such benefits until critical mass is achieved, until the creature can think about a variety of things in ways that will enhance its well-being. Therefore, off-line thinking cannot have been selected for per se, because until it achieved critical mass it would have been more of an evolutionary liability than an asset.

Off-line thinking could have been bootstrapped by something other than protolanguage, but we would then have to conclude that *two separate and distinct processes* required *two separate and distinct sets of cells* with the connective properties described, rather than a single set. But for the second hypothetical bootstrapper we have neither empirical evidence nor any sound theoretical motivation — only the reluctance of most behavioral scientists to accept a linguistic origin for nonlinguistic behaviors. Accordingly, we should not needlessly multiply entities by hypothesizing any second bootstrapper.

We are thus left with only three theoretical possibilities. (1) Thought created language as a cultural artifact. This is quite impossible, since language is obviously biological. (2) (Proto)language led to the creation of distinctively human thought as a cultural artifact. Equally impossible, since distinctively human thought occurs in all human societies to an approximately equal extent, therefore it too must be biological. And the only alternative left: (3) The same biological mechanisms, developed by and for language, run both distinctively human thought and language. This is the right solution, but it may not be a popular one.

The opposition to language as an engine of thought

There exists a long tradition of attempts to dethrone language from its preeminence in the life of our species, and particularly from any major role in human thinking. One must recognize, however, that such attempts may be natural and even appropriate reactions to some previous accounts of how language and thought interact—accounts that were misguided, or inexplicit, or couched in terms that could easily be misunderstood.

Typical of this widespread skepticism is British mathematician Roger Penrose (1989), who says "I, myself, simply cannot believe the common claim that ordinary human language is necessary for thought or for consciousness." Penrose's skepticism seems to be based on two grounds. First, he cites claims by several well-known scientists that they think in images rather than words. As should be clear by now, it makes no sense to say that people think either in words or in images. People think in electrochemical impulses, which at some (very late, perhaps even postfinal) stage of the thinking process may be converted into words or images at will. A predilection for either over the other cannot stand as evidence of what people do when they think.

The statement that someone "thinks in words" or "thinks in images" implies that we have some kind of privileged access to all levels of brain activity. This is an illegitimate assumption. We have no "need to know" how our thinking gets done, any more than we have a need to know how we metabolize our food, circulate our blood, create grammatical sentences, or do any of the myriad other things that our brains manage to get done for us without help from our conscious attention. There are many levels of brain activity involved in off-line thinking: it's an iceberg, and we are lucky if we can see one-ninth of its bulk exposed.

Penrose's second ground for disbelieving that language is necessary for thought relies on the work of neurologist Michael Gazzaniga, best known for his innovative research with split-brain patients. I have discussed Gazzaniga's findings at some length elsewhere (Bickerton 1990: 212–16), so I don't want to treat them in detail here. The main support for his position is that one of his patients, J.W., had a "rich language system" in the right hemisphere, yet that hemisphere could not "make a simple inference," and accordingly, "other systems" must be responsible for this. In fact, none of Gazzaniga's patients ever had a rich language system in the right hemisphere; at best they had a crude and limited form of protolanguage. Gazzaniga admits that J.W.'s right brain does not understand "syntactic niceties" but claims that, since it has a storehouse of words, language cannot be responsible for logical thinking, in particular for the forming of inferences (1985:97–99).

Gazzaniga does not take into account that any inference engine must be syntactical; that is, it must be able to put ideas together not merely in order but in an order that will directly, automatically, and unambiguously spell out answers to questions like: What is being done? Who or what is doing it? Who or what is it being done to? In other words, the inference engine must somehow supply exactly the information that syntax supplies. How could you construct an inference chain linking *pin*, *finger*, and *bleed* (one of the tasks J.W. failed on),[7] unless you knew that the implicit action was one of *pricking*; that the pin and not the finger served as the instrument by which the pricking was done; that the finger and not the pin was what got pricked; and that as a result of the pricking, bleeding would occur? But this is exactly the information that is conveyed, automatically and in terms of linguistic structure, by the sentence, "If you prick your FINGER with a PIN, it will BLEED." The logical conclusion of Gazzaniga's argument would be that the human brain includes two distinct mechanisms for the production of identical effects, even though the second mechanism cannot be specified—in other words, a flagrant violation of parsimony.

Gazzaniga's position is also vulnerable from an evolutionary perspective. At what stage of evolution did his hypothesized "other systems" come into existence? Here "other systems" advocates are on the horns of a dilemma. Either such systems preexisted humans or they came into existence when humans did. Assume that they preexisted humans. Then, if these "other systems . . . do the serious computing and decision making," species immediately ancestral to us should have had cognitive powers little if at all inferior to ours. But it is abundantly clear from the fossil record that they did not. If we assume that these other systems came into existence only with the birth of our species, at the same time that language did, such an evolutionary bonanza is wholly without precedent in the preceding three and a half billion years. So whether these systems preceded or accompanied the birth of our species, the results are equally implausible from the standpoint of evolution.

Next, let's consider some objections of philosopher Patricia Churchland (1986) and psycholinguist Steven Pinker (1992; Pinker and Bloom

---

7. What happened in Gazzaniga's experiment was that when the words *pin* and *finger* were presented to J.W.'s left visual field, he was required to choose a logically connected word (in this case, *bleed*) from a short list placed in front of him.

1990). Both deny that thinking crucially involves language, although from differing viewpoints and with differing assumptions. Pinker assumes that "human knowledge and reasoning . . . is couched in a 'language of thought' that is distinct from external languages such as English or Japanese" (Pinker and Bloom 1990:712). Churchland assumes we don't think in mentalese, precisely because she regards mentalese as simply equivalent to language.

Churchland's position is based on several misconceptions about language. "Language is a social art, and linguistic behavior serves a communicative function," she claims, for "Language is principally a device for communication" (1986:388). We saw what was wrong with that view in Chapter 1. Moreover she assumes that if you see human thought as mediated by language you *must* believe that *all* intelligent behavior by *any* species requires some form of mentalese, "the language of thought." She then proceeds to reduce this straw man to absurdity by asking us to hypothesize infants, orangutans, or even octopi equipped with mentalese.

The objection loses its force when faced with the division of thinking into "on-line" and "off-line." Many creatures (including infants, orangutans, and octopi) practice on-line thinking, and this is by definition intelligent activity. It differs from off-line thinking only in that the units which on-line thinking manipulates are the representations of objects immediately accessible to the senses, rather than more abstract representations (usually of objects not immediately accessible to the senses) that are quasi-permanently stored in the brain. Even human infants, however, show no signs of practicing off-line thinking.

But what about adults "without language"? Churchland asks us to consider the hypothetical case of a "nonverbal deaf-mute" unjustly committed to an asylum who makes his escape "after what must have been elaborate planning, deception and arranging." But Churchland is wrong in thinking that such a person is "without language." Presumably (if deafness is unaccompanied by other deficits, as the escape suggests) the "deaf-mute" possesses a normal human brain. Such a brain must come equipped with the wiring for language, the potential capacity to represent linguistic concepts, and the workspace for putting together such concepts in terms of Agents, Patients, Goals, and so forth—things essential for forming inferences, as we saw in connection with Gazzaniga's experiments. The fact that these mechanisms lack their normal input and/or output functions does not mean that such mechanisms are absent, and indeed the person's rational behavior suggests otherwise.[8] Thus the "deaf-mute" would be predicted to have an adequate off-line thinking capacity.

A similar equation of "inability to produce language" with "lack of language" pervades Donald's (1991:82–89) account of "Brother John," an epileptic monk whose severest seizures would result in the apparent loss of all linguistic capacities, although his general cognitive capacities remained intact (see comments in Bickerton 1993). Here again there is no reason to suppose that loss of the use of peripheral, input-output processes would in any way affect the permanent underlying mechanisms on which language depends. Indeed, there is less reason to suppose such things than there was in the deaf-mute case, since Brother John had normal and complete control of all language processes in the intervals between seizures. Clearly those underlying mechanisms did not mysteriously disappear and reappear, but remained perfectly intact during the temporary interruption of their external functions.

Deprived of support from this and similar cases, claims by Churchland, Donald, and others that language cannot be central to cognitive processing simply collapse. Pinker's approach is, however, somewhat different, and merits separate consideration. Pinker, unlike Churchland, accepts the proposal of Fodor (1975) that there is a "language of thought," a form of mentalese with its own syntax and semantics that preexists language and without which no language could be acquired. According to Pinker (1992): "Bickerton [1990] only provides an evolutionary scenario for the latter—for a system of 'mentalese' or 'conceptual structure' or 'language of thought'. . . . Bickerton has failed to provide an account for the evolution of natural *language*. Indeed, most cognitive scientists would insist that mentalese and natural *languages* are distinct systems" (emphasis added).

As this passage suggests, Pinker's argument depends crucially on a confusion between language and languages (a confusion he shares with a large number of other writers). It is easy enough to fall into the trap of using *language* as a generic term for languages, in just the same way as

8. Note that severe Down's syndrome can leave both input and output mechanisms intact yet victims are incapable of either coherent language or coherent thought.

we use *car* as a generic for all cars, or *book* as a generic for all books. There is, however, a significant difference. There is no such thing as "the car" or "the book": it must be some particular kind of car or some particular type of book. There is no biological or genetic car or book of which extant cars and books are just realizations. However, the argument of this book is precisely that "language" has just this kind of status: it is a human-species-specific faculty that exists separately and apart from its instantiation in any of the five-thousand-odd human languages.

That this is the case is illustrated by the nature of creole languages (Bickerton 1981, 1988, etc.). Such languages have emerged on several dozen occasions in different parts of the world, thus obviating the possibility that they could result from the dissemination of any preexisting language. They have arisen in situations where children were exposed to a variety of languages plus an unstructured jargon or pidgin—a version of protolanguage, in fact; examples of the latter from Hawaii, collected by Julian Roberts, are included in Appendix A. Children so exposed produced a novel language which drew much of its lexical material from the jargon or pidgin but also contained elements not found in any language or protolanguage to which the children had been exposed. Precisely those common elements occur repeatedly in creole languages all over the world. The only possible conclusion is that humans have an independent, preformed language faculty that need only be dressed out in words to provide a full-fledged language. It is already structurally complete, and does not require well-formed input, or parameter setting, or any of the desiderata assumed by students of language acquisition (Pinker 1984, Berwick 1985, Lightfoot 1989, etc.).

Indeed when Pinker, in a later work, comes to deal at greater length with his mentalese /natural-language opposition, the confusion becomes obvious. He (1993:78–82) gives a series of reasons why we cannot think in English: because English contains ambiguous expressions like *stud tires out*, because the same individual may be referred to in different ways (*the tall blond man with one black shoe, the man,* or simply *he*), because *Sam sprayed paint onto the wall, Sam sprayed the wall with paint, Paint was sprayed onto the wall by Sam,* and *The wall was sprayed with paint by Sam* all refer to the same event, and so on. We know that the four *Sam* sentences mean the same thing, but how would some mechanical thinking process running on English become aware of this? Pinker seems to fear that if he allowed the thinking process to know such things, he would be introducing the dreaded Cartesian homunculus into his account of mental operations; he seems unaware that if he claims *we* can know *anything* that our thinking processes cannot, he himself is introducing the homunculus in the guise of *we* (who and what *we* really are will form a topic of the next chapter).

So what lets us know that the four sentences are synonymous? According to Pinker, we can relate all four of them to a mentalese representation that looks like:

(Sam spray paint) cause (paint go to (on wall))

For the innocent reader to whom this might still look pretty English, Pinker adds that we should not "take the English words seriously"— presumably we could substitute abstract concepts of some kind for those words. (As is common in such arguments, Pinker makes the foundationless assumption that we can have abstract concepts that are quite unrelated to our possession of language.)

Fine so far. Obviously we do not want a species-specific thinking mechanism that depends on the morphophonemic shapes of English. But when you strip off those superficial disguises, what does Pinker's mentalese sample consist of? Something that makes use of linguistic concepts (undressed words) and that specifies thematic relations (*Sam* sprays *paint*, it's not *paint* sprays *Sam*; *paint*, a Patient, goes on *wall*, a Goal, not vice versa) in terms of structural relations (we know how the thematic roles are distributed because of the order in which the words are arranged) as well as specifying the logical relationships that obtain between different actions or events (it's *Sam spraying the paint* that makes *the paint go on the wall*, and not vice versa). In other words—no pun intended!—this mentalese is just syntax plus (some sort of) a lexicon. Is Pinker claiming that there is a syntax for "mentalese" and a syntax for "natural languages," and that these are totally different things? Why would evolution be so unparsimonious? But the nicest thing of all is that, given that creoles are the closest kinds of "natural language" to Language-with-a-big-L, you would expect this piece of mentalese to translate almost word for word into a creole. And it does:

Sam spray di paint mek di paint go 'pan di wall

is a synonymous and perfectly well-formed sentence in Guyanese Creole!

Pinker (loc. cit.) tells us that "mentalese must be simpler than spoken languages" because among other things "conversation-specific words and constructions (like *a* and *the*) are absent." But here Pinker misleads his readers. The words *a* and *the* do indeed have conversational *uses*: *the* may suggest that the identity of the referent of the following noun should be known to the hearer; *a* may assume that it is not. But these words are not conversation-*specific*, because they express lots of other things too, including knowledge that the individual thinker must take into account: for instance whether the referent is real and unique ("*The* President arrived here yesterday") or imaginary ("People would support *a* President who lowered taxes"); whether the referent is a category ("*The* Weimaraner is a kind of dog") or any individual member of that category ("*A* Weimaraner would make a nice present for Nancy"—she sure wouldn't welcome the entire breed!); and so on. Obviously the concepts expressed by the articles in these sentences must be expressed *somehow* in mentalese if the thoughts that correspond to the sentences are to be thought. Indeed, if we are thinking how we would present a piece of information to a hearer, even the *conversational* uses of articles must be available to mentalese!

Pinker attributes his mentalese sample to Jackendoff (1987), and indeed Jackendoff is perhaps the most sophisticated of the thinkers who would demote language to a purely ancillary role in thought. But, as suggested earlier in this chapter, the flaw in Jackendoff's reasoning is his failure to perceive any kind of discontinuity in the evolutionary development of cognition. In his own words: "The processes that we generally call 'rational thought' are computations over conceptual structures which exist independently of language and must in fact be present in nonlinguistic organisms" (1987:323).

In other words, Jackendoff sees human thinking as on a continuum with nonhuman thinking. He thus deprives himself of any explanation for why the outcomes of human thinking are so different from the outcomes of thinking in any nonlinguistic organism. How is it that the outcomes of nonhuman thinking affect only the immediate behavior of the thinker, whereas the outcomes of human thinking disturb and distort, not merely whole human communities, but the ecosystem itself? In Jackendoff's account, this difference is merely quantitative: humans think more/better/more radically than nonhumans. But the results do not differ quantitatively; they differ in kind. Human thinking possesses capacities wholly outside the range of nonhuman thinking; it changes the world, while the latter does not even change the individual.

It should perhaps be pointed out that there is a natural bias in favor of *continuism* (the idea that there is no radical discontinuity between humans and other species) that is shared by behavioral and cognitive scientists, if for somewhat different reasons.

Cognitive scientists are not, for the most part, interested in evolution. Many, perhaps most of them, concern themselves exclusively with human cognition; some concern themselves with animal cognition; very few specifically compare the cognition of humans and animals. Among those who do, there is a tendency to see too many rather than too few discontinuities (recall Donald's "mimesis" and Premack's "imaginal code"); McPhail was one of the handful who got the right number (one). But the majority of cognitivists believe that they can do their job by looking at one species (usually ours) and by treating cognition globally (after all, it's just computation).

As for behavioral scientists (and perhaps some cognitivists too), very many of them accept as a Darwinian article of faith that there can be no discontinuity between humans and other creatures. But the naïve observer may well ask how people who ride jet planes, read and send e-mail, then come home at night and listen to the messages on their answering machine before slipping a videotape into the VCR can seriously believe that their species is on a continuum with other species. I think the answer is this: one of the oldest and most reliable of human strategies is throwing the baby out with the bathwater. The bathwater that such thinkers wish to throw out is the Judeo-Christian belief that humans are different from and superior to other creatures because God created them separately and divinely ordained that they should be so. The baby in this case is the lamentable fact that, cut it how you will, we *are* radically different from other species, and to deny it (while eating a microwaved dinner or riding in a mass-produced auto) is hypocrisy. We are different, not because God specially made us so, not even because it is better so—it is perfectly possible to believe we are different and to wish we were not. We are different because evolution made us that way, because (for perfectly valid evolutionary reasons) it provided us, but no other species, with language.

But let us look more closely at how Jackendoff reached his position. He began his career with a major focus on semantics (1972), and although largely responsible for one of the most significant developments in syntax, X-bar theory (1977), most of his subsequent work (e.g., 1975, 1976, 1980) was devoted to semantics and led directly to his influential *Semantics and Cognition* (1983). Here he concluded that "the terms semantic structure and conceptual structure denote the same level of representation" (1983:95). Since he had already defined conceptual structure as "a *single* level of mental representation . . . at which linguistic, sensory, and motor information are compatible" (1983:17, original emphasis) there is no room in his theory for any other (i.e., nonsemantic) level of representation.

The formalism in which Jackendoff represents the contents of conceptual structure is similar to the formulae of symbolic logic, but his approach is richer and in several ways different. For example, a sentence like *Amy relinquished the doll* would be represented as:

[LET ([AMY], [GO   ([DOLL], [FROM   ([AMY])])])]

               Poss   Poss

As will be apparent, this resembles, although it is not identical with, the labeled bracketing by which syntacticians often represent the constituent structure of sentences:

[[Amy]   [[relinquished]   [the [doll]]]]

S NP   VP V   NP

So, just as with Pinker's example above, "conceptual structure" contains not only semantic information: it also expresses thematic relations (concepts like Agent, Goal, Source, and the like) and structural relations (that is, hierarchical relations such as "argument of," "head of," "modifier of," and the like). Thematic and structural relations represent, of course, the core materials from which syntax is made. What conceptual structure does not express (or expresses accidentally, because of the linear, two-dimensional form inescapable in written materials) includes the linear ordering of words into sentences and the morphophonemic shapes that linguistic concepts must take on if they are going to be used communicatively between two individuals.

In other words, conceptual structure contains just those elements that are universal (Language-with-a-big-L) and excludes just those elements that are language particular. And one might accordingly suppose that the next logical step would be to say that since conceptual structure contains the core elements of language, and conceptual structure is what we think with, then what we think with is language, period.

Why doesn't Jackendoff make this move? Well, suppose I am driving down a busy street and need to make a left turn. While I am waiting to make that turn, my brain must (if I am to preserve my homeostasis!) compute the velocity of, and distance between, oncoming vehicles, estimate the amount of time required to make the turn, and match these two calculations. Do I need language to do this? Surely not! This is an example of what Jackendoff would call "spatial cognition," and it relies on the experiences of untold millennia in which my ancestors, hominid, mammalian, even reptilian, had to accurately estimate distances and trajectories if they were to survive (and obviously only the ones that were better at it, in any given generation, could be my ancestors!). Is it rational thought? It had better be! This process is clearly a computation made over a set of representations, and those representations are not linguistic representations. But Jackendoff has already decided that there's only a *single level* of mental representation, so if language is not involved in *some* computational processes, it cannot be involved in *any* computational processes.

This is a logical consequence of Jackendoff's argument, but not one we are obliged to share with him. Where he goes wrong is by failing to distinguish between on-line and off-line thinking. My left turn, along with all the evasive and opportunistic behaviors of eons of nonhuman ancestors, was a case of on-line thinking. It computed over the immediate representations of things whizzing toward and past me, not over the much more abstract representations of the persons and events I was likely to meet and witness at the committee meeting I was on my way to. It is not so much that there are two *levels* of conceptual structure, rather that there are *two places* where computations can be carried out,[9] and

9. The term *place* should be taken with caution, of course. The last thing I want to suggest is some simplistic off-line thinking in the left brain, on-line in the right dichotomy. There are many more sophisticated ways in which types of computation could be spatially separated in the brain: perhaps by functionally distinct, even if structurally overlapping, neural networks. We simply do not know enough to say, at this stage.

Ironically, at one point Jackendoff comes very close to the on-line/off-line distinction, when (1987:265–67) he discusses "varieties of thought," informally

two *kinds* of representation—one much more abstract than the other. Even though what might seem to be the same thing is often represented in both places and in both ways, it does not follow that those two representations can both be used in a given computational process.

Jackendoff's stance is a Gertrude Steinian one: a representation is a representation is a representation. But not all representations are computationally equal. Consider the representations in Figure 3.2, where the same numbers are expressed in Roman numerals, English orthography, and Arabic numerals.

Qua representations, we would have to say that all three represent the same numbers, and as long as we leave computation out of it, there is no way of determining whether one representation is better or worse than the others. Romans got along just fine with their system of representation; they built the biggest empire of their day. But when you apply the simplest mathematical processes, you quickly find that there is no algorithm for dealing with the Roman or English orthography representations. There are simple straightforward algorithms for the Arabic representations, but the others just won't compute.

What I am suggesting is that primary (sensory) representations, whether in humans or other creatures, are like the Roman or orthographic representations of number: they are just too cluttered up with arbitrary and irrelevant detail to serve as units in computational processes that are off-line—that is, not concerned with immediately happening external events. On the other hand, only secondary (linguistic) representations, unique to humans, have the lean, stripped quality of the Arabic numerals—the "just a catness," the degree of abstraction already discussed in these pages—that enables them to serve in off-line processes.

Failure to make the on-line/off-line distinction causes Jackendoff numerous problems. He refrains from saying how far back down the phyla he thinks "conceptual structure" goes. This gets him into trouble right

---

distinguishing "fast" and "slow" processes, and mentioning Gardner's (1983) distinction between "bodily-kinaesthetic" and "personal" intelligence. In general, on-line processes are fast and off-line processes are slow, although speed is not really what distinguishes them. Gardner's distinctions are more orthogonal, although there is probably considerable overlap between bodily-kinaesthetic and on-line, as between personal and off-line. However, Jackendoff's discussion is in the context of Fodor's (1983) distinction between "central" and "modular" processes, and he does not pursue this line of inquiry.

Figure 3.2

Computable and noncomputable representations

XXXIV	plus			Thirty-four	plus
<u>XIX</u>	equals			<u>nineteen</u>	equals
?????				??????????	
		34	plus		
		<u>19</u>	equals		
		53			
XXXIV	times			Thirty-four	times
<u>XIX</u>	equals			<u>nineteen</u>	equals
?????				??????????	
		34	times		
		<u>19</u>	equals		
		306			
		<u>340</u>			
		646			

away with the ape-language issue, which he mentions but does not discuss (Jackendoff 1987:90). If apes have conceptual structure and if conceptual structure is so syntaxlike (having essentially all syntactic ingredients except linear ordering and morphology), why should apes be totally incapable of acquiring syntax? If they have conceptual representations that are anything like the *Amy* and *Sam* examples above—even if those representations are claimed to be simpler in some still-undefined sense—how is it that they cannot simply map the signs or words their trainers teach them onto those representations to yield grammatical sentences?

Moreover, the problems get worse the further back you go in evolution. Can a syntaxlike conceptual structure be shared by all creatures? Surely not by paramecia, or even nematodes! But where does it start, and what caused it to start? To say that "a computational description [of simpler organisms] is not very revealing" (Jackendoff 1987:31) does not get one off that particular hook. And all these problems, of course, are additional to the most serious problem with Jackendoff's formulation— its inability to account for the qualitative differences between ape and human intelligence.

It's not just that apes cannot do high-flying stuff like philosophy, science, or math; they are unable to tap dance, draw representationally, carry a tune, beat out a rhythm, or play simple card games—things that small children do either quite spontaneously or with a minimum of training. And yet when you look at what they *can* do, it is not impressively greater than what dolphins or even seals or African grey parrots can do, when you allow for the constraints placed on those other animals' behaviors by their physiology. But for primitive drawing you need abstract categories, for tap dancing and drum beating you need recursive processes: things that happen to be central to language, but unnecessary for the kinds of thing—even the intelligent kinds of thing—that other creatures do.

But one of the strongest counterindications to Jackendoff's position is raised, in his most recent work (1994:203), by Jackendoff himself. There, he admits that "unlike language, music, or vision, though, we have not been able to show that there are specialized brain areas for conceptual thought." This is surely a remarkable fact. The areas devoted to those other faculties have been recognized for some time, and although much remains to be learned about them, much is known. If *nothing* is known of *any* area "specialized . . . for conceptual thought," then Jackendoff's assumption that the discovery of such areas "awaits a more mature neuroscience" constitutes a blind leap of faith from an arbitrary position. The material surveyed in this chapter points to a quite different conclusion: that the reason these specialized areas have not yet been found is that they do not exist, and that all conceptual thought is carried out by the language areas in concert with other specialized areas of the brain.

None of this is meant to disparage Jackendoff's profoundly valuable work on what he calls conceptual structure. To the contrary, all that one needs to make his account compatible with mine is to introduce the on-line/off-line distinction and rename conceptual structure "Language-with-a-big-L." Remaining differences relate to the concept of consciousness, and I'll get back to these in the next chapter.

Final thoughts on thought and language

Perhaps we can grasp the relationship between language and typically human thinking if we think of the organism that produces both of them as being rather like a single factory. The single factory, however, does not produce a single product. It is like an automotive factory that produces cars, trucks, and tractors. It started off building a crude Model T type of car, and things just broadened out from there. Let us assume that all these vehicles share the same engine, one a bit more sophisticated than what powered the Model T. On today's production line, the engines are assembled first. At the point where the construction of the engines is complete, the production line divides. Off to the left go the engines intended for tractors; all they need is a tough chassis, some wheels, and a place for the driver to sit, and they're ready to roll. Down the middle go the engines for the trucks; these need a more complex chassis, a walled bed, a covered cab. Off to the right go the engines for the cars; these get a still fancier chassis, full bodywork, upholstery, automatic windows, you name it. But the engine is no different from the engines that power the tractor and the truck.

The tractor is nonverbal, off-line thinking; the truck is verbalized thought, such as I'm using as I write this, with its word order, morphology, and so on all in place, but minus phonology and intonation; the car is spoken or signed language as we utter and understand it in everyday exchanges. The engine is Jackendoff's "conceptual structure," my "Language-with-a-big-L": the stock of linguistic concepts and the core processes of syntax, which takes those concepts, assigns them thematic roles, and arranges them hierarchically in head-modifier and verb-argument structures so that it is made unambiguously clear (as it must be in thought, just as in language) who does what, and with which, and to whom.[10]

10. One possible objection to the model proposed here is that, in contrast with much current work in psycholinguistics, it concentrates on the production of sentences and largely ignores their comprehension. There is a reason for this. Although it is widely assumed that syntactic knowledge is always employed in sentence comprehension, this assumption is somewhat questionable. Work by Herman (Herman et al. 1984) indicates that dolphins are capable of responding correctly to numerous and quite complex sets of instructions, for many of which they have had no specific training. Similar capacities have been demonstrated for Kanzi the pigmy chimpanzee (Greenfield and Savage-Rumbaugh 1991). Yet not many linguists would be prepared to grant syntactic capacity to dolphins or pigmy chimps. More striking still, robots (Winograd 1972, Raphael 1976, Nilsson 1984) have shown themselves equally capable of responding to complex instructions. Probably no one would want to claim that robots have syntactic capacity. Moreover, it is significant that robots, dolphins, and chimps all labor under the disadvantage that they cannot produce sentences (Terrace et al. 1979).

Note that the mechanisms described above are assumed to be unique to our species and absent from even our immediate predecessors, *erectus* and the Neanderthals. But they could not have existed had not a million or two years of protolanguage amassed an adequate stock of linguistic concepts for them to work with. For it is the mechanism's sorting of such concepts into elaborate and predictable structures (whether tacit, as in thought, or overt, as in speech and sign) that has made possible the countless novelties our species has achieved.

Moreover, it should now be clearer how our remote ancestors could have had protolanguage so long with so little obvious benefit, even though protolanguage made off-line thinking possible *in principle*. Having protolanguage without the syntactic engine was like having gasoline without an internal combustion engine; there was not much you could do with it except sit around and wait for the engine to be invented— for the brain in its continued weaving and unweaving of connections to make just the right links for the syntactic network. You could use the equivalent of a kiddy tricycle: you could say "X did Y" or "Z did W," but you could not say "If X does Y, Z will do W" or "The X that did Y to V did W to Z, too" or "Whether X does Y or W makes no difference provided Z does U." You had more than any other animal, but you were still up a long, long creek with only a spoon for a paddle until the engine came along. Then you were off and running along the chartless route whose end is still not in sight but behind whose every bend unimaginable dangers lurk.

There *are* sentences (of a type more common in linguistic discussions than in normal conversation) that require to be parsed syntactically before they can be understood: for instance, *The boy kicked the dog that bit the cat* as opposed to *The boy that kicked the dog bit the cat*. However, the fact that *some* sentences have to be parsed in this way to be correctly understood does not entail that *all* sentences have to be; a sentenced like *Go to the refrigerator and get the orange*, uttered in a foreign language, could probably be understood by someone who had no inkling of that language's structural properties and knew only its equivalents of "go," "refrigerator," "get," and "orange"—indeed, it might well be figured out by one who knew only a couple of these words. Even if it proved to be the case that all humans do parse all sentences, in languages they control (they obviously cannot in languages they don't control), the argument would still stand. For it would still be *possible* for humans to understand some sentences *without* parsing, and those are just the kinds of sentence that organisms without syntax (from Kanzi on down) *can* understand.

Could this same engine that gave us language, off-line thinking, and a unique form of intelligence have also given us another of the features that distinguish us from other species—the peculiar form of consciousness that seems to many the true essence of what it is like to be human? That question will form the topic of the final chapter of this book.

Chapter 4

Language and consciousness

In the history of human thought, nothing has proven more intractable than the nature of mind. To many it has seemed self-evident that each of us contains an element that somehow escapes the physical laws governing the rest of creation. It was all very well to claim, with Lucretius, that nothing exists but atoms and the void, and therefore everything in the universe consists of matter and only of matter. But what was material about thoughts, beliefs, desires, dislikes? Such things felt as real to us as any physical object—perhaps even (in a sense exploited by idealist philosophers) *more* real. For our senses could be fooled, and could be shown to have been fooled, but how could we ever prove ourselves mistaken about things to which we seemed to have an even more direct mode of access? Who, if not ourselves, could tell us how we felt? Such things as desires, beliefs, and so on, insubstantial though they might appear, even seemed to have causative effects upon the world of material objects. Surely, then, these internal phenomena and our awareness of them must arise from mechanisms beyond the reach of "normal" science.

The weight of scientific opinion has gone against such views. All the achievements of science have come from the denial of mysterious essences or other nonphysical objects, and nowhere has its progress been obstructed or even delayed by the discovery of data that put this denial in doubt. To the contrary, if anything has delayed the progress of science it has been the unwillingness of some scientists to wholly abandon metaphysical assumptions. (Just within the field of evolutionary studies, one need only recall Darwin's original reluctance to publish, Wallace's insistence that humans fell somehow outside of evolutionary theory, and the persistence of belief in some Bergsonian *élan vital* as the driving force behind evolution.) The most natural conclusion is the one that has been drawn by a large majority among both philosophers and scientists: just as other mysteries of nature have yielded to a materialist approach, so will the mysteries of mind and consciousness.

Consciousness and the materialists

A common view is that consciousness is an emergent property that appears whenever brains achieve the right degree of complexity. But a brain, according to the same school of thought, is just a machine that carries out computational processes. It follows that there can be no principled distinction between brains and computers. Computers, just like brains, could achieve consciousness, and we would have to regard the conscious self, in the words of Daniel Dennett (1991:430), as merely "the program that runs on your brain's computer."[1]

Dennett is, of course, one of the most distinguished victims of Computer-Assisted Pygmalionism, or the CAP syndrome for short. Pygmalion, you will recall, was the legendary Greek sculptor who carved a statue so beautiful that he immediately fell in love with it. To be able to do this he presumably had to believe that he and the statue were organisms of a similar kind. CAP victims likewise believe that computers and human brains are organisms of the same kind, with similar ingredients (hardware, software) and similar computational functions. The brain's hardware consists of its neurons, their connecting axons, dendrites and synapses, and the overall architecture that determines what connects with what. The brain's software consists of all the data collected by our sense organs in the course of our lives, the patterns in which those data are stored and accessed, and the abstract recipes for behavioral routines that are based on those data.

Any differences that might seem to distinguish brains from computers are dismissed by CAP syndrome victims as irrelevant, temporary, or illusory. One irrelevant difference lies in the nature of the hardware. Brain hardware is organic, computer hardware metallic, but according to Paul Churchland (1984), "this difference is no more relevant to the question of conscious intelligence than is a difference in blood type or skin color." One temporary difference lies in the respective architectures of brains and computers. Computers are serial processors but brains are parallel processors, facts which differentiate the kinds of task for which each is best equipped. However, a current and quite feasible goal of the artificial intelligence community is the creation of parallel-processing computers.

Even this difference may turn out to be illusory, rather than temporary. Dennett (1991) has pointed out, quite correctly, that although the human *brain* is a parallel processor, human *consciousness* is a serial processor. Although our brains can carry out countless functions

---

1. I presume Dennett means by this, "on the computer that *is* your brain," rather than "on the computer that *belongs to* your brain," else we are back in the Cartesian theater with a vengeance!

simultaneously, we cannot be conscious of more than one at a time (James 1890:409—see note 9, below, for a rather different approach). Indeed, of many of these functions we can never be conscious at all. Recall from the previous chapter the experience of driving to work while mentally rehearsing a future committee meeting. While so engaged, we were not consciously aware of our driving, although this must have been carried out with some degree of skill if we incurred neither traffic tickets nor accidents. Then a ball bounced into the road, and the immediate environment filled our consciousness, erasing—at least from our awareness, probably not from unconscious computation—the meeting rehearsal that a moment ago had monopolized our attention. One can hardly doubt that consciousness arises in some way from the operations of the brain, but unlike the brain, it cannot focus on many things at once, or even on just two things at once.

No matter how things finally come out, everyone who has ever thought about mind and consciousness owes a profound debt to what is often called the "strong A.I." (artificial intelligence) position—the position so ably presented by writers such as Dennett and Churchland. The claim that computers could (at least in principle) achieve consciousness has stopped a great deal of amiable waffling about the mind, and forced those of us not yet afflicted by the CAP syndrome to clean up our act. In particular, Dennett (1991), following Ryle (1949), presents perhaps the most thoroughgoing attempt yet to banish forever what he calls the Cartesian theater—belief in the self as a metaphysical essence within a material brain, the homuncular spectator for whose benefit the senses put on their lively and vivid spectacles.

How well has the challenge of strong A.I. been met, so far? Not very well. Perhaps the most cogent, certainly the most argued-over attempt at a rebuttal is a thought experiment by philosopher John Searle (1980, 1982, 1988) known as the Chinese Room. Searle asks us to imagine a hand-simulated version of a computer, fully capable of passing the Turing test (Turing 1950). When questions written in Chinese characters are passed into the room, the room responds with answers appropriate enough to convince a Chinese speaker that the room actually understands Chinese. In fact, all that the room contains is Searle himself (who knows not a word of Chinese), a pile of Chinese characters, and a list of printed instructions that enable Searle to choose the characters that spell out appropriate answers and then pass those answers through a slot in the door of the room.

According to Searle, this thought experiment falsifies the strong A.I. view that computers can have mind and consciousness. For one feature of mind is the ability to understand languages, including (at least potentially) Chinese. But neither Searle nor anything else in the room understands Chinese.

To which the strong A.I. response is, "Well, the whole room is what understands Chinese" (Hofstadter and Dennett 1981). As a linguist I do not find this response unreasonable. I have no idea whether the Chinese Room could understand Chinese, but that is simply because nobody knows how one understands Chinese or any other natural language. The process could be as purely mechanical as whatever it is that goes on in the Chinese Room.[2]

It's true that, among humans, understanding Chinese may be accompanied by a *quale*, a subjective feeling along the lines of, "Gee whiz, I can understand Chinese, and this is what it feels like to understand Chinese, and no mechanical device could feel that." But subjective feelings of this nature are altogether unreliable. There are no privileged positions, and therefore no privileged reporting. In a wide variety of ways—through optical illusions, posthypnotic commands, studies of brain states resulting from traumas or the ingestion of illegal substances—it can be demonstrated that subjective feelings about personal experiences often prove wildly at variance with the truth. If this is so under abnormal stimuli, what guarantee do we have that our subjective feelings are any less misleading under normal ones?

The problem with arguments about the strong A.I. position on consciousness is a familiar one. As with countless other issues, interested parties line up on one side or the other. Those who feel that the strong A.I. position does not contain the ultimate truth attack it mercilessly. Strong A.I. supporters, convinced (and not without reason) that these attacks lack force and that the attackers have no concrete alternative to

2. Dennett makes the valid point (1991:436–40) that Searle avoids explicating the degree of complexity in what must go on there if the room is to pass the Turing test—something, at the very least, far too complex and too rapid for Searle to hand simulate, in real time, with any degree of conviction.

offer, defend their position as is, without feeling any need to examine it critically. What has ensued is a stalemate that has existed for the last few decades, ever since the question of consciousness resurfaced from the debacle of hardcore behaviorism and became respectable again.

How can that stalemate be resolved? Obviously, not by more of the to-and-froing we have seen so far. One side needs to develop its position in some way. And that side has to be the strong A.I. side, regardless of what one might feel about it, for the simplest of reasons: the opponents of strong A.I. have not produced any explanation of consciousness that is amenable to development.[3] Strong A.I., on the other hand, has made some fairly specific proposals about what might underlie consciousness: the nature, arrangement, and mode of functioning of the perfectly familiar, everyday, nonsubatomic neurons and their connections that inhabit our brains. Such proposals are unacceptable as currently stated, for reasons to be given shortly. However, this does not mean that they cannot be made acceptable by the factoring-in of additional elements.

Consciousness-1

In this book I have been looking at everything through the twin lenses of evolution and behavior, because by so doing, one seems to cut through a great deal of muddle. Long before anything could have been said to have a brain or intelligence or even senses, amoeba-sized creatures were struggling to achieve homeostasis: that is, they tried to maintain any condition—warm or cold, dark or light, rich in one chemical or in another—that would favor their continued existence. We do not have to hypothesize any mysterious Life Force to account for this. Merely suppose that, in the beginning, there were creatures that tried to prolong their lives, creatures that tried to shorten them, and creatures that didn't care one way or the other. Which group's progeny could be expected to populate the world a few billion years later?[4]

---

3. Proposals such as the "psychons" of Eccles (1990) or the "quantum mechanics" of Penrose (1989) have of their very nature to be rejected or swallowed whole. They do not, at least in any obvious way, seem to welcome modification—while other approaches make even less tangible suggestions.

4. The distinctions between forms of consciousness elaborated in the pages that follow strongly resemble some made by Dennett (1969; see also Arbib 1972, Dennett 1978). I was unfortunately unaware of this when I wrote this section, but feel that a point-by-point comparison of our views would disrupt the flow of

Maintaining homeostasis means responding to the environment. Moving from shade to sun, or vice versa, is just one example of this kind of activity. But you can't respond to sunlight without awareness that the sunlight is there. Clearly, this awareness is consciousness, of a kind—maybe not the kind that we seem subjectively to enjoy, but still worthy of the name; anyway, let's call it Consciousness-1. What is Consciousness-1 consciousness of? Well, things in the environment, obviously, or else creatures could not respond appropriately to changes in light intensity, the appearance of potential predators, prey, or mates, together with other homeostasis-threatening or homeostasis-enhancing experiences.

Consciousness-1 does not come as an all-or-nothing package. It will vary in degree across species in much the same way as animal intelligence seems to do. As noted in the previous chapter, wide variations in sensory capacity and response plasticity contribute to the illusion of a *scala naturae* of intelligence, where in reality there may be no more than two levels below the third level of language. Similarly, one may derive the impression that there is a *scala naturae* of consciousness. After all, when *Escherichia coli* demonstrates awareness of a glucose molecule by moving toward it, one need not suppose that it recognizes, even tacitly, whether that molecule is the same as or different from the glucose molecule it encountered yesterday, or even that it distinguishes glucose molecules from galactose molecules, either of which it can metabolize (Donachie 1979). Conversely, rats that have been made sick by evil-smelling water (Garcia and Koelling 1966) immediately recognize a second presentation of that water and refuse to drink it. Thus other aspects of brain function, such as memory, may interact with Consciousness-1 so it appears to have greater breadth and depth in some species than in others.[5] But these

---

exposition and distract the reader from the particular points I wanted to make. Interested readers are therefore invited to make their own comparisons between the two models. However, it is not insignificant that Dennett and I, approaching the issues from completely different viewpoints, should agree on as many points as we do.

5. However, it is worth noting an ingenious experiment subsequently performed by Garcia and his colleagues (Bermudez-Rattoni, Forthman, Sanchez, Perez, and Garcia 1988) in which rats, after ingesting "sweet-tasting" water, were first anaesthetized and then injected with a substance that causes nausea in conscious animals. The subsequent refusal by the rats to drink sweet-tasting water suggests that *sleeping versus waking may be irrelevant to Consciousness-1*, which will go on

differences of range, due to the progressive interaction of other modules, provide no basis for denying the essential unity of Consciousness-1.

It should be emphasized, however, that Consciousness-1 is not limited to consciousness of things in the external environment. Take proprioception, the feedback from one's own actions and internal states. This still involves external phenomena (external to the brain, that is), but here the external object is the creature's own body. All creatures above a pretty low level of neural sophistication have circuits that provide them with information about their own movements. The claws of a crab could not converge on a moving shrimp if the crab's brain did not receive a constant stream of information, not only about the movement of the shrimp but about the movement of its own claws. A hawk could not reliably connect with a moving rabbit without massive feedback from the hawk's own body yielding data on velocity and distance and angle of descent. The last of these (the only one over which the hawk has any control) must change as the rabbit moves, but cannot change appropriately unless the previous two (plus the speed and direction of the rabbit) are factored into the unconscious, on-line computation that the hawk must carry out in order to achieve its goal. To this extent, if no further, creatures must be conscious of self. But at best this is an on-line consciousness, an awareness of a string of immediate events that need not, and probably does not, spill over into the generalized, looking-before-and-after kind of consciousness with which we humans are so familiar.

Then in addition there's pain, a purely internal, self-bounded experience, even though occasioned in many cases by some external factor. It used to be claimed that many creatures felt no pain, a convenient excuse for vivisectors. Pain, however, constitutes such a valuable aid to homeostasis, prompting rapid withdrawal from a wide variety of potentially destructive entities and events, that we would expect it to be widely distributed among species. Pain is, of course, an on-line experience: we may remember past pain, and dread future pain, but the pains we remember and dread are mere abstract symbols for the incommunicable, irreproducible experience itself. But that experience is clearly subjective:

---

functioning for as long as any cells capable of responding to external stimuli remain in working order. In this analysis, only Consciousness-2 would be interrupted by sleep, and even that not very efficiently, since we dream!

normal individuals could not possibly suppose that the pain might be outside themselves, or that it might belong to someone else.

Thus the boundary between Consciousness-1 and our kind of consciousness does not coincide with the boundary between subjective and objective experience. Consciousness-1, as the foregoing clearly indicates, is both objective and subjective. The distinction can be more plausibly attributed to a factor already shown as playing a significant role in human behavior: the distinction between on-line and off-line processing.

A position in some respects similar to that presented here has been advanced by Gerald Edelman (1989), who actually used the term "primary consciousness," and pointed out some of its limitations: an animal possessing primary consciousness, even though learning might alter its behavior, "has no means of reviewing explicitly its present perceptions in terms of analogues in the past or in terms of anticipated analogues projected to the future. It has no direct awareness . . . and is not 'conscious of being conscious'" (Edelman 1989:186). It is, of course, precisely this consciousness of being conscious that most strikingly embodies what it is like to be human, and accordingly to this we now turn.

Consciousness-2

First, however, it may be appropriate to ask whether we are being too parsimonious in denying to other creatures any form of consciousness more elaborate than Consciousness-1. I don't think so.[6] Consciousness-1 is concerned solely with on-line processing; in other words, it mediates between a nervous system and the rest of nature. What our kind of consciousness (call it Consciousness-2) does is to provide us with awareness of Consciousness-1. We not only see the rabbit; we know that we are seeing the rabbit. But Consciousness-1 is wholly absorbed in the task of mediation. Indeed, you might better say that Consciousness-1 *is* the

6. The behavior of apes (Gallup 1982, Menzel et al. 1985) is often cited as evidence that they possess a consciousness of self equal (or similar) to ours. However, the fact that apes may recognize (parts of) themselves in mirrors or on television monitors does not necessarily entail that they have *the same awareness of their own internal experiences* as we have. Indeed, it doesn't even entail that they have internal experiences—but simply that they have the associational capacity to link the stimulus of a movement of their own fingers, lips, or whatever with the stimulus of an identical movement visible in the mirror or on the screen.

task of mediation, no more, no less: it consists, purely and simply, of everything that enables us or any other creature to know that there is a world there at all. Accordingly, there is nothing *in* Consciousness-1 that could make it conscious of itself, as well as of the world it mediates. For consciousness of consciousness to arise there would have to be (and here we return again to the central theme of this book) some part of the brain that is to some extent detached from this incessant traffic between brain and environment.

In other words, the creation of human consciousness depended on the creation of areas of the brain from which the workings of animal consciousness could be objectively perceived. And, as we saw in previous chapters, only the emergence of language could have created such areas of the brain. If, as Jackendoff (1987:325) claims, "the higher animals likely have levels of representation something like ours," why should there be such a tremendous disparity between what we and those "higher animals" are able to do, computationally speaking, with those representations?

Coming from an entirely different direction, A.I. expert Marvin Minsky (1985:58) anticipated the general position of this book several years ago when he wrote the following recipe for producing a self-conscious organism: "Divide the brain into two parts, A and B. Connect the A-brain's inputs and outputs to the real world—so it can sense what happens there. But don't connect the B-brain to the outer world at all: instead, connect it so that the A-brain is the B-brain's world." If this sounds familiar to readers of Bickerton (1990), let me assure them that I hadn't read Minsky's book when I wrote it—like fins, tail flukes, and preparedness for language, this is a genuine case of convergence, not a homology. But clearly, with a minor disclaimer or so, Minsky's A-brain is equivalent to my Primary Representational System (PRS), and his B-brain to my Secondary Representational System (SRS). I just wouldn't be quite so sure that the B-brain/SRS is as self-encapsulated as Minsky's phrasing suggests.

Minsky's model, however, worried Dennett (1991:313), who feared that it could be construed as licensing a single presentation process to a single, homuncular observer; he points out, quite rightly, that "There doesn't have to be a *single* place where the Presentation [of conscious experience, DB] happens." But neither Minsky nor I would dream of claiming that there was such a place, any more than Dennett would dream of claiming that potentially conscious information is diffused throughout the brain, including those areas that regulate respiration, metabolism, and blood flow.[7] Indeed, if the area of the brain devoted to consciousness were not severely circumscribed, what would be the point of all the internal processing mechanisms that handle sensory input? We are not conscious of the raw input into our retinas, nor indeed of anything along the complex route that visual information follows, until its processing is complete (but see the remarks on blindsight in the section entitled "Some Puzzles of Consciousness," below).

What happens is that information is received by one part of the nervous system, processed by another, then sent to yet other parts, where it engages in Darwinian competition (Calvin 1987, 1989) with the outputs of further processing areas. Indeed, even this picture is far too neat, since areas are often poorly demarcated and intercalated one with another in ways that we are only just beginning to sort out. As for the maxi-regions, the A-brain/PRS and the B-brain/SRS, these are, for sure, equally jumbled together, and demarcated only by their patterns of connectivity. In many respects, too, their structures and modes of operation are similar: both contain cohorts of neurons that fire simultaneously at certain stimuli; both are divided into modules which, while they possess a degree of autonomy, have to cooperate with other modules to perform their various functions, and so on. However, the B-brain/SRS does not receive (or does not receive many) stimuli directly from the environment, but does so indirectly, through the A-brain/PRS.

To recapitulate, then: all creatures, ourselves included, enjoy Consciousness-1, awareness of ourselves and our surroundings, to a widely varying degree of richness: poorly in simple organisms, quite thoroughly in some of the more complex ones. However, Consciousness-1 is an on-line operation, unceasingly involved in the moment-to-moment exigencies of existence. Consciousness-2, consciousness of one's own consciousness, can come only in a species some of whose brain areas are

---

7. Dennett does not explicitly propose any internal division of the brain comparable to mine or Minsky's; however, he has pointed out (personal communication) that his thought experiment with the Vorsetzer—an imaginary device that reads images produced by a computer-aided design (CAD) system (Dennett 1991:291ff.) was intended to show, in a slightly different context, that different parts of the brain can present material to one another without in any way requiring a homuncular observer.

exempt from this immediate environmental traffic and can scan the behavior of areas of primary consciousness as objectively as the latter scan the environment. Without language, it is doubtful whether those exempt areas could ever have come into existence.

But does this mean that Consciousness-2 is linguistic consciousness, that it entails, or consists of, the capacity to say, "Yes, I am conscious of myself, and this is what it feels like"? Well, yes and no. Let's begin by spelling out the yes option.

Consciousness-3?

There are grounds for supposing that there is indeed a Consciousness-3 and that it is in some special sense linguistic. A brain both aware of its own awareness and possessed of language cannot merely feel pain (Consciousness-1) and experience itself feeling pain (Consciousness-2) but can also announce, "I have a pain in my big toe." Steven Pinker (1992) has pointed out that "availability of information to some central processor in control of reporting" is not the same as "subjective experience of sentience ('what it is like' to see red or to feel pain)" and that neither are the same as "an ability to know and reason about oneself (self-consciousness)." He's right—of course they're not. However, it does not follow from this that they are clearly distinct and separate things with no significant connections between them. To the contrary, all forms and levels of consciousness are linked in a web of mutual entailment.

You cannot report on a subjective experience without having a subjective experience to report on (or without believing you have, which, since subjective experiences are hard to verify objectively, in practice amounts to the same thing). In other words, although Consciousness-1 can exist without Consciousness-2, Consciousness-2 logically entails Consciousness-1. But what about the difference between subjective experience of pain and being able to say, "I have a pain"?

In principle, the two could be independent. It is quite possible to conceive of a creature that could experience pain, could be aware that it was experiencing pain, but had absolutely no means of telling anyone that it was experiencing pain ("the availability of information to some central processor in control of reporting"). Whether or not any central processor was involved, there might just be nothing to report *with*. And we can by no means be sure that creatures such as I have described, in reduced numbers, of course, are not walking around us at this very moment.

Perhaps we would not have reduced their numbers so drastically had we suspected that they suffered anguish in exactly the same way that we did, and lacked merely the capacity to tell us about it.

But could apes really be just such conscious but uncommunicative creatures? It seems doubtful at best. To have a Consciousness-2 (awareness of awareness) without a Consciousness-3 (ability to report same) would still entail the existence of a B-brain, an area within the brain free from constant brain-environment traffic within which awareness of awareness could arise. But how could such an area have been created, if not by the emergence of language?

This is, of course, a "what else?" argument—of necessity vulnerable to any demonstration that something else does exist and could plausibly have produced the necessary effects. However, so far as I know, there are at present no candidates, no other necessarily off-line processes that would have been adaptive enough to fix genetically in face of the heavy energy expenditure that the addition of large numbers of brain cells entails. Surely the emergence of consciousness itself could not have been responsible for adding these brain cells. For why should Consciousness-2 have emerged of its own accord? Without the language that enables us to make use of it, Consciousness-2 (mere awareness of being aware) seems to have no adaptive value. One could even argue that it might prove maladaptive, intensifying fears and inhibiting action to a degree that might interfere with homeostasis.

None of this denies the possibility that on another planet, under quite different circumstances, a plausible candidate might exist—a creature that felt, and knew that it felt, but couldn't tell you what it felt. However, no evidence suggests that such a creature exists on our planet. And if, on our planet, Consciousness-2 must be accompanied by language, then any creature equipped with "subjective experience of sentience" must ipso facto have "availability of information to . . . reporting." At the same time, it seems equally implausible to suggest the converse disjunction: a species that had language but was not conscious. Certainly no such species exists here, and there would seem little likelihood that it exists on other planets, for the following reason: language as we know it entails the capacity to talk about anything under the sun, including our own actions and perceptions, which we could hardly discuss objectively if we were not conscious-2 of them. Thus, though Consciousness-2 and Consciousness-3 may be distinguishable, they mutually entail one another.

But what about the "ability to know and reason about oneself"? Here we confront what may to many seem the most central phenomenon of being conscious in the way humans feel themselves to be conscious, as well as the intuitive, subjective ground on which the persistence of dualism is largely based. There *has to be* something responsible for this feeling—even if the feeling could be mathematically proven to be an illusion, *we would still need an explanation for why we had this particular illusion rather than some other illusion.*

But the feeling, vivid as it is, seems on closer examination too para-doxical to be true. For if it is "oneself," one's *whole* self, that "one" knows and reasons about, what is it that does the reasoning and knowing, and what is reasoned about and known? I have no trouble with reflexive behavior as long as I am talking about *physical actions.* When I look at myself in a mirror, my eyes perceive an image of the front part of my body; when I scratch myself, my fingernails contact part of my skin; when I hurt myself, some action of my body causes pain to a particular part of that body. But what happens when I know myself, respect myself, despise myself, remind myself, and so on and so forth?

Our sense that we can indeed do these things, that it is not non-sensical to talk about them, is surely founded on *some* kind of dividing line in the brain—a line that need not be absolute, need not even be permanently fixed, but should in some sense distinguish processes we normally have access to from those to which we normally don't. Dennett is perfectly right in his insistence that this line cannot be drawn round some central homunculus, lording it over the rest of the brain. But what is proposed here is far different from that: simply that one of the numerous ways in which we can divide up the functions of the brain has certain consequences for how the world appears to that brain. One part gets information firsthand, the other secondhand. (This explains the time lag that can be shown to exist between the two; see Dennett's [1991] discussion of Orwellian and Stalinesque explanations of false memories, or the title of Edelman's [1989] book, *The Remembered Present.*) One part is conscious of the output of the other, but not of its internal workings, so that one part can be reported on, the other cannot.

There may indeed be three (or more) separate *senses of the word* "con-sciousness," even if we exclude Consciousness-1. But this in no way entails that there are three *kinds* of consciousness peculiar to humans. On the contrary, there is only one kind (what I have called Consciousness-2) with (at least) three aspects, or consequences: that we can be aware of our awareness, that we can report it, and that we can submit it to some form of analysis ("know[ing] and reason[ing] about oneself"). But it should be emphasized that these consequences are not consequences of one another, either, and in a different kind of being might not come as a package. They come as a package in our species because our species has language. If a species has language, it can hardly fail to be aware of its own awareness; joint possession of language and Consciousness-2 then entail the capacity to report and logically analyze that awareness.

However, if it makes people happier, they can talk about Consciousness-1 and Consciousness-2/3, insofar as human consciousness includes reportorial and analytic functions that can be distinguished from what a pure Consciousness-2 (mere consciousness of Consciousness-1) would provide. And indeed one could argue that for some purposes it makes sense to talk about Consciousness-3, a purely linguistic consciousness. For, as we shall see, the possession of language gives a unique spin to the way we see ourselves, and goes a long way to account for the intuitive appeal of dualism. Indeed, it may be entirely responsible for the fact that we see ourselves as selves at all.[8]

The inevitable invention of the self

Let's start from the reporting of experience. Suppose you say to me, "I have a pain in my big toe." This is a bizarre statement, from several viewpoints.

8. Once again it is instructive to compare the present proposals with those of Edelman (1989). Edelman sees that what is crucial to the development of (in my terms) Consciousness 2/3 is the evolution of "structures that allow a *symbolic* modeling of the self-nonself distinction" (original emphasis). He adds: "Such structures free some part of neural activity from the external drive of current behavior at the same time that this part still retains access to that behavior and its consequences"—just as proposed here. However, while admitting that "All of these properties are also those needed in the exercise of a true language," he draws a conclusion the exact opposite of what has been drawn here: that "the development of . . . language is absolutely predicated on the existence of consciousness"—not just primary consciousness but also forms of (nonlinguistic) symbolic representation (Edelman 1989:186–87). This conclusion, however, is based on a severely defective understanding of language (1989, chap. 11) and a failure (while paying them lip service) to really grapple with biological and evolutionary considerations at any significant level.

First of all, "I" doesn't really mean you, at least not in the sense that "Mary Bloggs" means Mary Bloggs. It only means you for as long as you are talking. When I am talking, "I" is me and you are "you." When I and somebody else are talking, you are "he" or "she." "I" is a signal to indicate who is doing the talking. "You" is a signal to indicate who is being talked to, and "he," "she," and "they" are signals to indicate who is being talked about. In other words, pronouns are simply a device for regulating discourse, like the hand signs police make when a power outage obliges them to direct traffic at intersections. The police, hopefully, make the traffic flow smoothly; the pronouns, usually, make the discourse flow smoothly. Occasionally we have to say things like, "When you said 'he,' did you mean Bill or Joe?" (and in many languages, people must have to say things like, "When you said [third person singular], did you mean Bill, Mary, or the dishwasher?"). But with "you" and "I," the linchpins of discourse, there is never any ambiguity.

The trouble is that every time *I* use "I" it means "me," one particular exemplar of the species *Homo sapiens sapiens*. And this is just as true when I spin internal soliloquies (and when, in consequence, there is no "you" to swap roles with) as when I engage in conversation with others. In consequence, although "I" should not by rights aspire to more than traffic-signal status, it inevitably becomes, for me (as for every other "I") the self-identifying label that I use whenever "I" want to know, or reason about, "myself." So, equally inevitably, "I" develops into the full-blown hero of a narrative lasting a lifetime—a hero with a host of "his" or "her" unique attributes and particularities, every bit as real as any hero of any novel you ever read.

This kind of co-option of "I" seems to have been inevitable from the moment that language (or protolanguage, for that matter) began. How could anyone get by, in talking or thinking, if there was no distinctive label for the talker or thinker? Yet in a book still taken surprisingly seriously in many quarters, Jaynes (1976) claimed (mainly on the basis of an uneasy liaison between split-brain theories and conventions in classical literature) that human self-consciousness as we know it developed less than four thousand years ago. However, in several languages we actually know what the morphophonemic form for the first person singular was at that and at still earlier periods, while in many more languages, first-person-singular forms can be reliably reconstructed for periods earlier still. One can only wonder who or what Jaynes thinks our ancestors of five thousand years ago thought they were referring to when they used their equivalents of "I."

The ubiquity of "I" has a variety of consequences. In English (and in many other languages) we have no way of avoiding utterances such as "I have a pain." What does this really mean? If I have an umbrella, an assistant, an uncle, or a drink, then umbrella, assistant, uncle, and drink are all entities quite separate from me. If I have a pain, that pain is just part of me. Nor is there any escape in those languages that have to say things like "Pain is in me" or "Pain catches me"; they make a similar distinction between me and my pain. Likewise with "my arm," "my leg," "my cold," and a whole variety of things which language distinguishes from my essential self. Indeed, mind-body dualism is endemic in language, only to be conquered by a wrenching of the mind even more extreme than that which occurred when the "natural" perception that the earth was flat collided with the unfortunate fact that it is actually round. The flat-earth belief was not enshrined in language, and indeed not all sensory evidence confirmed it (e.g., ships disappearing below the horizon). But with "I," the mechanisms of language conspire with subjective convictions whose roots lie deeper than sense—spring, indeed, from just those experiences of "our" desires, beliefs, feelings, and so on that seem to provide evidence even more direct and compelling than sensory evidence.

Note that more than the mere discourse necessity of "I" is involved here. Dualism follows too from the subject-predicate distinction that is fundamental to all language, even to protolanguage. Instead of holistic descriptions, "bird-flying," "cow-chewing," and so on, we are obliged to separate an actor or topic from an action, an event, or a state: "The bird flew," "The cows chew," and so on. Thus even the replacement of "I" by our own names (a practice attempted by many young children) would not free us from dualism. It would still be a case of "Joe Blow says this, does that, has a pain, has a belief" and so on and so forth.

Once you divide an individual into, on the one hand, this totally independent "I," and on the other, everything that this "I" supposedly possesses (pains, colds, arms and legs, mothers and mothers-in-law, desires, intuitions, opinions) and everything that this "I" does, you guarantee a dualistic view of the self. If only we had some neutral way to speak of things! But we don't, we must soldier on with the language biology gave us. And since language is indeed biological, rather than cultural, hell will probably freeze over long before we can get language to accept that we are what we do and do what we are, and that any line drawn between our being and our doing can only be a misleading fiction.

Until that improbable day, what I say (and therefore feel) that I am will continue to be the proud possessor of this all but infinite set of properties (colds, mothers-in-law, opinions . . .). What I intuitively feel myself to be will remain a web made up of stunningly different types of property (mental phenomena, physical phenomena, attributions by others, abstract relationships, and so on) that are somehow held together to yield the illusion of a single self-conscious self. What holds this web together? Could it be the same factor that gives conscious experience another of its characteristic features—its single, serial, one-thing-at-a-time nature?

Attention

First let's summarize where we're at. Self-consciousness as we know it is simply Consciousness-2 plus language. Consciousness-2 necessarily includes Consciousness-1, because Consciousness-2 simply *is* consciousness of Consciousness-1. Now the primary purpose of Consciousness-1 is homeostasis. In order to ensure homeostasis, Consciousness-1 has to determine, out of the Jamesian "blooming, buzzing confusion" that the senses present, just which features of the environment have the greatest likelihood of affecting the organism's homeostasis, positively or negatively. This entails a constant competition for consciousness, a natural selection process in which only the fittest (to help or to hurt) survive. From the stream of afferent signals along the various sensory and proprioceptive channels, an organism has to distinguish what it needs to attend to from what it can safely ignore if it is to balance its energy budget and maintain homeostasis.

Attention, neglected for a long period after the debacle of "introspectionist" psychology a century ago, has been treated extensively in recent years (e.g., Johnston and Dark 1986, Naatanen 1992, Posner and Rothbart 1992, and references therein). In all creatures above a fairly low level of development we find at least an orientation response and frequently full-blown attention mechanisms whose functioning is essential to their survival. Such mechanisms are geared above all to the perception of novel stimuli. Novel stimuli must be detected and assessed as soon as possible, because their appearance indicates a change in the environment, and any change has homeostasis-affecting potentialities. In creatures with any degree of complexity, a report of a novel stimulus on any sensory channel is relayed to an attention device that seeks to extract comparable information from the creature's memory store. There it either succeeds or fails to identify the stimulus with some known category or situation for which there exists already an appropriate response. Exactly how this matching process is achieved is interesting in itself but irrelevant to our present purposes.

If a stimulus can be matched in some way, appropriate motor action (and/or the inhibition of inappropriate action) is immediately triggered. If no identification can be achieved (if, in other words, the stimulus proves a truly novel one), the organism remains alert, with all available sensory channels focused on the stimulus, tracking it until one of several possible outcomes occurs: some change in the stimulus allows identification to take place; some change in the stimulus (involving a sudden approach, a loud noise, or some similarly alarming symptom) marks it as potentially dangerous, even if unidentified, in which case escape mechanisms will be activated; the stimulus disappears; the stimulus remains at the same level for some time. In the last two cases (and the first, if the stimulus is identified as harmless), attention ceases to focus on it and can be switched to any competing stimulus.

To function effectively, an attention mechanism can focus on only one thing at a time. This is not to say that other stimuli are ignored; they continue to be monitored, and can be upgraded at a millisecond's notice if they become more salient. But at any given moment, the mechanism's dedication must be undivided. An organism in an attentive state is poised on the brink of action, and that action, when it comes, must be equally undivided. The creature cannot simultaneously advance and back off, or freeze and assume an aggressive posture, no matter how conflicting the signals it receives (it can, of course, perform such actions *consecutively*, even in rapid succession, but that's a different story altogether).

Now we see why, as Dennett pointed out, the brain should resemble a parallel processor hooked up to a serial computer. The brain has to parallel process in order to be able to deal, on line, with an enormous amount of incoming information, and it has to serial process in order to extract the most currently relevant pieces of information and to act on them singlemindedly. This is true of all Consciousness-1 creatures, and the advent of Consciousness-2 does not change the situation. That advent does not equip us with an additional attention mechanism — why should it? Instead, it simply increases the domain over which the attention mechanism operates. Instead of its range being limited to the external environment, it now in addition automatically scans the internal workings of the brain. If there's nothing outside that has any immediate significance — no environmental threats or opportunities in the offing — the attention mechanism can switch inward, and indeed frequently does.

How does the attention mechanism select from the workings of the brain what it will attend to? As noted above, selection from external input seems to be largely determined by homeostatic needs. But once stimuli are coming from within the brain, it becomes much harder to determine the basis for selection. Part of the subjective feeling of consciousness is that "we" direct "our" thoughts to those areas which, for perfectly rational reasons, currently concern "us" the most. But enough has surely been said already to suggest that this is a post hoc rationalization. It is rather that those areas of our minds within the purview of consciousness remain in a constant state of Darwinian competition. Dozens, perhaps hundreds of topics struggle to replicate themselves (Calvin 1993) and drown out the voices of others by sheer weight of numbers. It's the squeakiest wheel that gets the grease of attention.

In many cases that wheel may prove violently dysfunctional. Stripped of its role as the watchdog of homeostasis, living in an environment created by a species powerful enough to tolerate a good deal of antibiological conduct (Bickerton 1990, chap. 9), the brain may obsess over the real or imagined sufferings of an irrecoverable past or lose itself in grandiose dreams of an unattainable future. Mental disturbance constitutes an abnormal mode of functioning that falls outside the scope of this book, but it seems worth mentioning that it is precisely the relative independence of Consciousness-2 from homeostasis-seeking interactions with the environment that allows (and perhaps actually fosters, through feedback loops) the development of dysfunctional thought and, in many cases, behavior. Such dysfunctions simply constitute the inevitable downside of the vast increment in computational power that off-line areas of the brain provided.

Returning to the serial, one-thing-at-a-time nature of consciousness, it is worth noting that the undividedness of the attention mechanism[9] does not represent the sole cause of that nature, which is also powerfully abetted by the nature of language. Indeed, this is only what we would expect, given that language originally created the off-line areas of the brain, the only areas to which we have conscious access—given, too, that normally whatever we are "conscious-2" of can be verbally expressed, and vice versa. Language is irremediably a serial, one-sound/syllable/morpheme-at-a-time process, and this is not merely because of the nature of the vocal channel through which its expression is most often forced. Sign language could potentially transmit two or more streams of information at once, but does not exploit this potentiality.[10]

9. Note that although it is a commonplace idiom to ask people to give their undivided attention, nobody really expects anyone to be attending to two things at the same time. Rather the idiom expresses a fear that the minds of hearers may periodically wander to other topics that will make them, for the time they are so occupied, quite unconscious of what one is saying.

However, in an interesting recent study, Searle (1993) has made a distinction between what he calls the "center" and the "periphery" of consciousness: "right now I am paying attention to the problem of describing consciousness but very little to the feeling of the shirt on my back or the tightness of my shoes. It is sometimes said that I am unconscious of these. But that is a mistake. The proof that they are a part of my conscious field is that I can at any moment shift my attention to them" (1993:10).

This is a problem for any theory which, like Searle's, regards consciousness as a single, unitary phenomenon. For the present approach, it is not. All the time that Searle is conscious-2 of his ideas about consciousness (on which his attention mechanism happens now to be concentrated), he is also conscious-1 of his tight shoes, his shirt, and probably many other things, such as the kid practicing the violin next door. Precisely because he is conscious-1 of them, and because his attention mechanism ranges over both domains of consciousness, it can turn at any moment to any of those other phenomena. However, it is wrong of Searle to say "that *I* can . . . shift *my* attention to them" (loc. cit., emphasis added). Who is this "I" that shifts attention, and whose attention gets shifted? What really happens is that Searle's new shoes start to press on a nerve, or the future Paderewski produces a clinker.

10. Among fluent users of American Sign Language, information equivalent to that supplied in spoken languages by pronouns or bound morphology can be conveyed by eye movements or direction of gaze or posture which occur simultaneously with the signs for lexical items. However, there are no subject-predicate signs (that is, unitary signs expressing such things as "bird-flying"), and although it should not be impossible in principle, no user of any sign language can carry on simultaneous conversations, one with the left hand and one with the right.

Some puzzles of consciousness

The model of consciousness sketched in preceding sections of this chapter helps to explain some puzzles of consciousness that have vexed philosophers and others who have considered its possible nature. Let us begin by returning once more to the familiar example of "unconscious" driving, referred to in this and the previous chapter. Everything we experience enters Consciousness-1, so we are conscious-1 of all of the other vehicles, cyclists, intersections, and other hazards we negotiate as we proceed. (If we hadn't been, we would have hit someone!) Moreover, there's no reason to suppose that these memories were immediately lost or extinguished. Dennett says (1991:137): "surely *if you had been probed* about what you had *just* seen at various moments on the drive, you would have had at least some sketchy details to report" (original emphasis; see also a similar account of the "unconscious-driving" experience in Dennett 1969:115–19). Naturally *if you had been probed*, you would (lacking any available response in Consciousness-2) immediately have directed your attention mechanism at the contents of Consciousness-1! And those contents don't have to be on-line simultaneously, so that "had just seen" proviso makes no difference. If the attention mechanism can dredge up memories of years ago (as it must, to match them with current experience), it can equally well dredge up memories of moments ago, even if one was quite unconscious of laying them down (see note 5 above).

How can "unconscious" memories be made available to consciousness? As is well known, the brain has usually more than one route for getting from one place to another. Let us suppose that the B-brain is not as encapsulated as Minsky proposed and that there is a direct route from vision to Consciousness-2 which can be kept open by the attention mechanism: when that mechanism is working you are consciously aware of what you are seeing, and when it isn't, you are unconsciously aware. In the first case, the information travels directly from X to Y; in the second, it takes the route that leads from X to Y via Z—only when it gets to Z, *it stops there!* There is no *automatic* transfer onward to Y. However, *if the attention mechanism is alerted* (as by Dennett's "probe," for example), Y can send a message: "Go to Z and fetch ?" (? being whatever is in Z). And, lo and behold, we "remember" what we had not been conscious of a moment before.

In fact, subjects under hypnosis can often recover memories of events that happened years previously. Obviously it would be absurd to suggest that everything that enters Consciousness-1 achieves a permanent record, but it seems plausible to suppose that everything receives a record *of some kind*, and our unconscious memories of events will degrade unequally just as our conscious ones do. Hypnotism simply acts as a probe, directing the attention mechanism to a specific area, but it has the added advantage that it cuts down on the competing chatter that goes on continually in the brain, and thus tends to minimize interference with the recovery task.[11]

Another puzzle involves the behavior of so-called split-brain subjects, persons who have undergone commisurotomy, the severing of the corpus callosum and other structures connecting the two hemispheres of the brain. Gazzaniga (1985:95ff.) reports an experiment in which words or pictures were flashed to the right brain of a subject, J.W. When asked what he had seen, J.W. denied having seen anything. When asked to draw what he had seen, J.W. initially refused the task as absurd, but on being told to just go ahead and draw *something* with his left hand, J.W. drew what he had just denied having seen.

In the present analysis, this is not as mysterious as it sounds. In the model just sketched, X (the cells in J.W.'s retina that respond to his left visual field) send information to Z (J.W.'s right visual cortex) but fail to transmit that information to Y (the consciousness-linked language area being interrogated by Gazzaniga) via the direct route, since this has been cut. Y reports, understandably, that nothing was seen. However, the information is there, in Z. Gazzaniga's insistence that J.W. report *something* activates and focuses J.W.'s attention mechanism. According to Posner and Rothbart (1992), the neural substrate for attention consists of a posterior attention network (both parietal lobes), an anterior attention network (anterior cingulate, supplementary motor area), and a vigilance

11. Naturally, in considering information recovered under hypnosis, one must always bear in mind the possibility of confabulation: the natural tendency among humans to fill in gaps in stories with plausible-sounding material. And undoubtedly, on some occasions, such confabulations have (quite accidentally) coincided with the truth, offering apparent powerful confirmation of the ability to recover "lost" information. However, the fact that *some* hypnotic memories are confabulations by no means provides evidence that *all* hypnotic memories are confabulations (see Hilgard 1965, chap. 8, for discussion).

network (right frontal). Presumably commands addressed verbally to a subject activate only left-hemisphere attention mechanisms. How would these communicate with the right hemisphere after commisurotomy?

If the operation was complete, all of the normal channels will have been cut, save for a very indirect one. The cerebellum lies below the two hemispheres, an older (although in humans a greatly augmented) area, and it has links to both hemispheres. Thus the right hemisphere can be alerted, but that doesn't necessarily mean that information about events known only to the right hemisphere can be sent back by the same route (or, even if it can be sent back, that it can be read by left-hemisphere language areas). If this is indeed the case, then alerting of right-hemisphere attention areas would allow J.W. to *draw* what he had seen, but only the physical emergence of his own drawing, now accessible to *both* visual fields, would enable him to *name* what he had seen—just the result that Gazzaniga obtained.

Another phenomenon, one that has attracted philosophers, psychologists, and neurologists alike, is that of blindsight (Weiskrantz 1986, Cowey and Stoerig 1992). This condition results from damage to the visual (occipital) cortex, creating a scotoma or blind spot in the patient's vision. Despite the fact that patients cannot consciously see anything within the area of this blind spot, they are often able to state, at rates well above chance, whether or not a light has been flashed in that area, or, if a simple shape has been presented, what that shape was. How are they able to do this?

Given the model of consciousness described above, blindsight ceases to be puzzling. The visual cortex is where visual information gets its final processing prior to being sent on to conscious areas of the brain: here is a case where to reach Y, information from X (in this case X is the retinal and other earlier processing stages) normally has to go through Z, the visual cortex. The fact that the information cannot be processed by Z means that Y cannot receive it (in its finished form) but not that X does not still have the same basic information in a relatively raw form. The problem is simply one of recovery, of "consciousness raising" (in the sense of raising *to* consciousness, rather than *of* it, of course). It is significant that blindsight patients, like commisurotomy patients, have to be prompted before they will give responses. Just as in the split-brain case, alerting the attention mechanism serves to activate the search for the missing information. It is significant that only relatively crude information (presence versus absence of stimuli, or basic shapes) is recoverable, indicating that an early stage of processing, not normally available to consciousness, is being tapped.[12]

Finally, let us turn to a fourth puzzle that has only recently begun to be investigated. English neuropsychologist Lorraine Tyler and her colleagues (1988, 1992; Tyler and Cobb 1987) have studied differences between the performances of aphasics in "implicit" and "explicit" tasks connected with language. An implicit task is one which requires some kind of internal knowledge representation but where that knowledge need not be conscious: for example, pushing a button whenever a particular word appears in a visually presented text. An explicit task is one in which knowledge has to be accessed consciously: for example, making a grammaticality judgment.[13]

The puzzle, in this case, arose from some aphasics who were originally diagnosed as having severely damaged language faculties yet who performed well on certain tests. Although they did quite badly on explicit tasks, they performed up to a normal level on implicit ones. For instance, latencies of response to the word *guitar* were measured when a patient RH was presented with four instances of the frame *The crowd was waiting eagerly. John . . . the guitar* in which the gap before *guitar* was filled with the verbs *carried, buried, drank,* and *slept* respectively (Tyler 1992:166ff.). The first of these texts is fully acceptable, the second pragmatically anomalous, the third violates selectional restrictions, and the fourth violates the subcategorization frame of the verb. For normal subjects, latencies are slower for all three of the anomalous sentences, indicating that they are subconsciously utilizing all the types of linguistic information involved,

---

12. The fact that only such blurred images are accessible under these conditions casts some doubt on Jackendoff's (1987) Intermediate-Level Theory of consciousness, in which he suggests that only what Marr (1982) termed the 2 1/2 D level of visual processing is accessible to consciousness. I prefer here the approach of Dennett (personal communication), who claims that "it is a mistake to think we can draw a probe-independent boundary" between different levels of consciousness (or, I would add, between different levels of processing, visual or nonvisual).

13. Note that the *basis* on which a grammaticality judgment is made may be at least partly unconscious. Naïve subjects seldom know *why* a given sentence is ungrammatical, and they are often wrong when they guess. In fact, grammaticality judgment is an example of what Ingvar (1990) has called "complex ideation," combining both conscious and unconscious processes.

and are aware—conscious-1 aware, that is—of the grammatical and other errors those sentences contain. RH's latencies were statistically indistinguishable from those of normal speakers, indicating that he too was subconsciously troubled (and his responses delayed accordingly) by all three types of anomaly. However, when RH was asked to make overt grammaticality judgments on sentences with similar anomalies (*John drank the guitar*, *John slept the guitar*, and suchlike), his performance fell well below that of normals.

Other tests of implicit and explicit language skills were given to RH and other subjects with similar results. Such results are not easy to reconcile with most approaches to consciousness, but they follow naturally from the approach detailed above. They suggest that in cases such as that of RH, underlying language processes remain partly or even fully functional, and that only conscious access to them is impaired. This implies just the kind of two-level type of consciousness that has been elaborated here. Tyler's own words (1992:175) are worth quoting: "The data described in this chapter suggest that consciousness (as it applies to language comprehension) is not a uniform phenomenon. . . . There are at least two types of awareness involved. . . . [T]hese two types of awareness come from different processes. One process which is automatic . . . and one which is under voluntary control (at least to a certain extent) and which involves reflection on the properties of the final representation. They can be selectively impaired in brain damage."

Thus all four of the areas surveyed above tend to confirm the validity of a dual-consciousness model. However, the foregoing account has been necessarily brief and sketchy and lacks any detailed description of how Consciousness-1 and Consciousness-2 interact with one another. It may therefore be useful to consider a practical illustration.

How consciousness works

Suppose you are walking alone down a dark street at night and a particular configuration of shadow falls on your retina. This pattern is carried deep into the brain, where it is processed. The attention mechanism immediately flags it as a novel (and potentially hazardous) stimulus and seeks for a match so that identification can be carried out. Within milliseconds a possible match is found: the pattern of shadow could represent a human figure.

So far, we're still on the level of Consciousness-1, in the A-brain. But, as Minsky remarked, "The A-brain is the B-brain's world," so that whatever is going on in the A-brain becomes a potential topic for Consciousness-2. If you were merely a Consciousness-1 creature you would probably continue down the street—more cautiously, perhaps—until you had achieved a better resolution of the image, or until the configuration of the image changed in some significant respect. However, while autonomic sensory mechanisms continue to scan the novel stimulus, prepared at any instant to call the attention mechanism back to the external world, that attention mechanism switches its focus to Consciousness-2.

But isn't this on-line functioning? Yes and no, mostly no. Yes, because it is directly triggered by an environmental stimulus. No, because it actively engages the areas of Consciousness-2, and because while it lasts, no action will issue from it; indeed, given certain outcomes, no action may ever issue from it. The attention mechanism, using all available resources of the SRS, is engaged in a process of analysis that is trying to make logical sense out of the stimulus. In so doing it follows a reasoning process in every way analogous to the processes that, under other circumstances, one might carry out in one's study or during spells of insomnia. That process proceeds thusly. The figure (if it is a figure) is not moving, suggesting that it is waiting for something. But there is no bus stop in the vicinity, no store window that might have attracted someone's gaze. What could the figure be waiting for?

Now the lexicon may come into play, for if we can find a straightforward linguistic description for what is going on ("waiting for someone to let him/her in," "walking a dog that's just gone behind a bush to relieve itself," or whatever), your brain can tell itself that it controls the situation. Whether the lexicon is used consciously or not will be determined by where the attention mechanism is right now. Has it returned to focus on the shadow (in which case the lexical search will be quite unconscious) or has it remained in off-line mode (in which case the lexical search will be quite deliberate and conscious)? Either way, let us assume that the word "lurking" appears, popping into consciousness magically and unexpectedly if the search was unconscious, or appearing as the logical end point of a rational inquiry if it was not. Who lurks by night? Thieves, muggers, and rapists do. The module that carried out the identification immediately shoots out an all-points bulletin: "Possible perpetrator! Perp alert! Action stations!"

You cross rapidly to the other side of the street and increase your pace. Your identification of the shadow as a human figure and the human figure as a potential perpetrator has not (or not yet) been contradicted by anything. It has therefore become a state. We have a name for identification states: that name is belief. You believe that the figure is a potential perpetrator, and this belief has modified your behavior (it is not the figure itself—if it even is a figure—that motivated you, but your interpretation of that figure). Does this mean that a mental event has caused a physical event, as the mind-body dualist might conclude? On one level, no. Some electrochemical events have triggered other electrochemical events, that's all. On this level, mind states are indeed equivalent to brain states, just as materialist philosophers would tell you.

On another level, however, things look somewhat different. Was it because of *the actual nature of those particular electrochemical events* that you crossed the street? Like, since neurons A, D, F, and G fired, you crossed the street, but if neurons A, B, E, and H had fired, you wouldn't have? If human minds really were like computers, this would indeed be the case, and the end of the story. If we were machines, the firing of the "perpetrator" cells would, given all the other objective parameter-settings of the situation (night rather than day, isolation rather than company, and so on) indubitably fire the "crossing the street" cells (or cells for some other appropriate behavioral equivalent). What kind of machine would we be if they didn't? For that matter, what kind of animal would we be if they didn't? A dead one, you might well think.

But in fact it was not really the firing of particular cells that caused our behavior. Rather it was the representations that those firings evoked, and the interactions between those representations and a host of other representations currently co-occupying the SRS. You might say, "Well, nothing surprising about that. Cells represent in the PRS, too. Some cells in a gazelle's PRS represent lions, and what makes the gazelle take off is not the fact that cells T, Y, and Z fired, but the fact that cells T, Y, and Z, firing at a particular rate, represent a charging lion." This is true, and this is how animals work, and this is how machines work, and this is how we work, a lot of the time. But not all the time. We, but not the others, can also work in a different mode.

Imagine, if you will, a gazelle with cells T, Y, and Z firing, and in full possession of all its physical faculties, that continued to graze peacefully as the lion hurtled toward it. If we were to see such a sight, how would we explain it? By saying that the gazelle had a death wish? Or believed in the inevitability of fate? Or was the victim of a lack of self-esteem and therefore saw all pain and suffering as deserved? Or was subject to delusions of immortality and omnipotence? These explanations sound absurd, but no more absurd than the scenario that provoked them.

Then what am I claiming? That creatures other than ourselves are mere automatons? Certainly not. Animals can and do exhibit autonomous behavior, modifying their responses in a variety of ways. A female with young offspring may decide to fight, rather than flee a predator. A monkey with close kin present will utter warning calls, whereas the same monkey with no kin present may not (Cheney and Seyfarth 1990). But these animals vary their behavior according to objective parameters (such as presence versus absence of young or close kin). They do not vary their behavior according to subjective parameters (beliefs, dispositions, emotional states, and so forth).

Does the lion-gazelle scenario sound absurdly unlikely when translated into human terms? "Rapun [an artillery officer, DB] left with two guns to find a new position. They [his unit, DB] stopped just outside the town of Barcena de Pie de Concha, where a sudden air attack caught them unprepared. Unlike the other men Rapun did not throw himself to the ground but remained sitting on a parapet. A bomb exploded nearby and he was mortally wounded" (Gibson 1989:471). Many people with military experience will have seen, or at least heard of, similar incidents. In this case, the victim's lover had been brutally murdered by a death squad a year previously.

The difference between other animals and ourselves is simply this: we have a vastly wider range of behaviors (wide enough to include self-destructive behaviors unknown among other species), and we have this range precisely because our behaviors can be determined, not by which neurons are involved, nor even by what particular neurons represent, but by interactions between what those different sets of neurons represent. And the liberty (relative, if not absolute) given us by this variety of possible behaviors—what use to be described, rather inaccurately, as "free will"—derives solely from the fact that, thanks to language, we were able to build up a store of internal representations exempt from immediate (but not always, as Lieutenant Rapun's fate reminds us, ultimate) physical consequences.

To give a specific example of how representations can interact to produce results that no simplistic brain-state equals mind-state formula could predict, let us return to the dark-street scenario and suppose that instead of being located, like most of us, somewhere on the average-to-timid range, you had a representation of yourself as tough and fearless, equal to any challenge. You might then, despite your belief that the shadow was a person and the person determined to do you harm, have continued to walk along the same side of the street, determined to kick the bejazus out of anyone who dared to interfere with you.

Now, your self-representation as a tough, fearless fellow quite clearly constitutes a mind state. What exactly is the brain state that corresponds to that mind state? Is there a bunch of neurons somewhere in your head, constantly chugging away, churning out "I am bold and fearless, I am bold and fearless, I am . . ." or its electrochemical equivalent? Or is it not more probable that anything so all-pervasive as one's concept of what kind of person one is is in no sense modular, but rather the emergent product of an infinite variety of preceding states and experiences—awareness of one's own physical size and strength, attitudes inculcated by parents or peers, memories of previous conflict situations satisfactorily resolved, choice of role models or hobbies . . . The list is endless.

Note that this kind of mind state, indeed any kind of mind state that involves self-image or self-evaluation, lies totally beyond the power of any computer to replicate (or for that matter of any animal—it's hard for us, outside of a nursery-tale context, to think of any lion thinking, "I am braver than all other lions!"). Is there the remotest possibility, not just now, but ever, that as you sit there punching in data, your Hewlett-Packard will be thinking, "Gee, I can lick anything IBM ever made!"? The reason the idea is absurd is because to have any kind of self-image you have not merely to possess a space to form images in and a means to represent them—you also have to be an individual. You can't be an individual if you are the 2,708th exemplar of Model XB-39579-C.

And yet, as we have seen, this computer-unattainable mind state can influence behavior like any other—can, in the case we have been considering, determine whether you will cross the street or not. You might still think, "Well, no matter how complex the brain states that give rise to self-images, one could still, *in principle*, find out just what is represented by every conceivable combination of neurons in someone's brain, and somehow deductively determine from them and their potential combinations what more general states they might give rise to." I think that is wildly overoptimistic, but just for the sake of argument we can concede that it might be possible. Could we then predict how the owner of the brain in question would respond to the possible-perpetrator identification in the dark-street scenario?

The answer is no, for a very simple reason. Out of all the countless representations in an individual's brain, there is no way, even in principle, that we could predict which would be triggered by any given occurrence. Take the case of the tough, fearless fellow who believes that the shadow is human and may mean harm but who walks on anyway. But what if that morning he had read a horoscope that told him this was an unlucky day for him. "Oh well," you reply, "we'd have known from our brain scans that he was superstitious, of course," But that wouldn't help unless we also had a moment-to-moment record of his experience; if he hadn't happened to read that particular horoscope (quite likely by chance), his superstition or lack of it wouldn't have been relevant to the situation. So in order to have any predictive power, our model of his brain states and their informational content would have to be updated on a 24-hour, 365-day basis.

Actually, things get a lot worse than this. Suppose that, like so many of us, he is superstitious and scornful of superstition by turns, or suppose that he is not normally superstitious but felt depressed about his job and had a bad cold the morning his eye happened to fall on the horoscope. And then, as he turns to cross the street, random neural activity triggers one of those memories on which his normal self-image is based. "Hey, what kind of wimp am I?" flashes across his mind, and he steps back onto the nearer pavement and continues as before.

Now there is no way we could have predicted he would do that, even with a 24-hour update, because here the stimulus was internal and randomly generated; consequently its probability of occurrence cannot be computed even in principle. What we have is the absolute indeterminacy of mental events. There's no need, like Penrose (1989), to invoke quantum mechanics to account for that indeterminacy. It arises and must arise wherever cohorts of neurons represent concepts of things in the world that do not need to be activated by the physical appearance of those things, and wherever those representations can interact with one another—in other words, in an SRS, something which, as far as we know, can only be created by and for language.

Machines revisited

Dennett really had his eye on the ball when he described the Self as "the Center of Narrative Gravity" (1991:410). In other words, we are whatever holds together the stories we construct about ourselves. But how can he then say, almost in the same breath (1991:430), "you are . . . the program that runs on your brain's computer" (or even its less provocative version, "that organization of information that has structured your body's control system"). "Has structured" gives the idea that it's a done deal, in the same sense that a computer program has to be a done deal, otherwise it's not much use as a program. Just imagine that when you punch in "quit," your terminal displays next week's engagements. Not always, just when it feels like it. And occasionally it reprints your last file instead. If you couldn't debug that program, you would junk it right away. Absolute indeterminacy has no place in a machine. However, as we saw in the last section, absolute indeterminacy is what the mind, of its very nature, has built into it.

But then even in the first, good definition there is a problem with the wording. The word "narrative" too might suggest a polished, rehearsed performance, but that is not all: it implies that what the mind constructs is a solo performance, Scheherazade spinning her yarns to a passive caliph. Surely a better metaphor for the self would be Center of *Dialogue* Gravity. For what the mind constructs is not a solo piece but a constant interaction between individual and environment—a story that not only edits itself but is edited by its surroundings in unpredictable ways as it unfolds. Whoever heard of a continually self-editing computer program— one that, untouched by human hand, generated entirely novel responses to the input data it received?

This interaction with the environment and the goal of homeostasis that the brain seeks not only produce many of the phenomena characteristic of consciousness but also mark two more crucial distinctions between human brains and computers. Computers do not interact with the environment. They sit on tables and desks and compute when you tell them to. So whatever they *can* do, they cannot make dialogue. There might be something they could make narrative with, but to make dialogue you need (at least) two parties. And since it is dialogue, not narrative, that creates the self, computers cannot have selves, and could not have them even if they were unique entities rather than the 2,708th exemplar of Model XB-39579-C. For self may be a fiction, as Dennett and I agree (fiction in the sense of artificially constructed character rather than untruth, of course) but perceiving that fiction, believing in it and being guided in our life choices by what it seems to be, form crucial ingredients of what it means to be conscious the way humans are. So on these grounds alone, computers could not achieve a consciousness like ours.

Similarly, computers are not seeking homeostasis. They have nothing to seek it with: no sense organs for detecting phenomena, no behavioral repertoire for responding to those phenomena. We have to seek homeostasis for them. It is we, not they, who dust them, cover them when not in use, control the temperature and humidity of the rooms in which they sit, use software that purges them of viruses, and attach them to surge suppressors so as to protect their internal representations. If we are delinquent in these duties they will suffer, but there is nothing they can do about it. Thus there is nothing for them to have consciousness *for* and nothing for them to have consciousness *with*. And since Consciousness-1 is for preserving homeostasis, they cannot even in principle have Consciousness-1. But if they cannot have Consciousness-1, and if our special consciousness, Consciousness-2, is merely consciousness of Consciousness-1, why would it ever occur to anyone that they could have Consciousness-2? Without an organism that actively seeks homeostasis, there can be no consciousness of any kind.

It follows from this that one of Dennett's ambitions (a tongue-in-cheek one, I hope) is unlikely to be realized. Dennett argues, quite logically, that if the self really is "the program that runs on your brain's computer," then "you could in principle survive the death of your body as intact as a program can survive the destruction of the computer on which it was created and first run" (1991:430). But this program is a constantly self-editing one that requires continuous interaction between the creature that created it and the environment in which that creature constantly seeks homeostasis. How, even in principle, at whatever stage of technological development, could such a program run on a medium that provided neither of these things? Even today's modest programs won't run on all machines. So the result of Dennett's new transmigration of souls would most likely be instant extinction—or at best, imprisonment in some virtual purgatory or electronic limbo.

After this it will probably come as a surprise if I say that I believe, in principle, that a conscious machine could be built. Indeed, Canadian philosopher Leonard Angel (1989) has produced a perfectly cogent recipe for such a machine. It would, of course, be a robot, not a computer. It would have to learn to forage, to avoid danger, to feel pain: in other words, to achieve homeostasis for itself. This should give it Consciousness-1. It would then acquire language, which when added to its other capacities should give it secondary representation, thus human-type thinking and Consciousness-2. I have, however, one word of advice: if anyone ever makes such a machine, grab a shotgun (12-gauge pump, for choice) and head for the hills, because our day will be over.

Consciousness summed up

All the evidence surveyed in this chapter supports a view of consciousness essentially dual in nature. One part consists of a level of awareness that we share with other creatures; and upon that level we, like they, can behave intelligently in a variety of ways. However, while we are aware *at* that level, we cannot, except in exceptional circumstances, be aware *of* that level (we are aware of its end products, naturally, but not of the level that produces them). The other kind of consciousness, what I have called Consciousness-2, can come about only if the brain has spaces in which off-line representations (internal representations that do not have to be triggered by environmental stimuli and do not necessarily provoke overt behavioral responses) can be stored and where, accordingly, off-line processes can be carried out. Here the results of Consciousness-1 can be made available for leisurely inspection (it is surely significant that conscious processes are generally many milliseconds slower than unconscious ones).

Note that I am not saying consciousness and language are the same thing (even though the extent of the overlap between things we are conscious of and things we can report on is impressive, to say the least). The *reductio* of Patricia Churchland (1986:390)—addressed to Fodor's (1975) "mentalese," although it might just as well be addressed to language—points out that, if all beliefs are sentences, people "must be credited with an infinite number of beliefs" stored in this form. Granted that her assumption is correct, her argument still cannot prevail against the present model. As Churchland herself says, "What is stored is generally something else, something that may be verbally encoded on demand, but need not be verbally encoded to be cognitively engaged. . . . [T]here is no reason to assume it must first acquire a sentential encoding" (1986:392).

Just as was pointed out in Chapter 3, while thought processes in general may (and while off-line processes must) exploit the earliest stages of syntactic processing, they need not (and, in many cases, cannot) undergo the later stages of that processing.

However, it remains the case that without language, areas disengaged from on-line processing (the necessary, and perhaps even sufficient, condition for off-line thought and consciousness) would probably not have developed, and the massive overlap noted above between conscious and reportable phenomena would therefore not exist. Churchland (1986:396) quotes approvingly the statement by Hooker (1975:217): "Language will surely be seen as a surface abstraction of much richer, more generalized processes in the cortex, a convenient condensation fed to the tongue and hand for social purposes." Cutting out the condescending last phrase, this is almost right, although perhaps not in the way the author intended. Language does indeed represent an abstraction from the rich, complex wealth of information that Consciousness-1 makes available—*but then so does Consciousness-2*! How much of what surrounds us, how much of what our senses dutifully record, remains inaccessible to our consciousness?—not to mention the wealth of information about our own internal processing that countless psychologists and psychoneurologists are struggling, not always with too much success, to make accessible to us!

Like old age, this state of affairs may seem deplorable until you think of the alternative—which in this case is not having any conscious knowledge at all of what goes on in the world. Consciousness may have no evolutionary function to fulfill, may (as I have suggested) be simply the epiphenomenal consequence of other faculties. Perhaps even our complex thought processes don't really require it: we could sit around, internal wheels whirring, then just jump up and do what was required without any more idea than the birds or the bees of why we were doing it. We would then be a very different species, of course, but not, perhaps, an impossible or even less efficient one. But what would our lives be worth to us without the royal feeling that we do not merely know, but know that we know—the feeling that we are both spectators at the Cartesian theater and heroes of the plays performed on its stage? Illusion though that be, isn't it fun?

Conclusion

In this book, I have presented a somewhat controversial thesis: that the emergence of language is the direct and root cause of all those mental characteristics that distinguish us from other creatures, particularly our special kind of intelligence and our special kind of consciousness, which between them generate modes of behavior not merely unknown among other species but utterly remote from anything we can find in other species. However, there are a couple of points that should be mentioned before closing.

Throughout this book, and quite deliberately and intentionally, I have concentrated on precisely those aspects of human behavior that differentiate us most clearly from other species—what one might call the behavioral apomorphies (features unique to a given species) of *Homo sapiens*. Such an approach is often taken as a claim that humans are beings totally separate from the rest of nature. It is, of course, nothing of the sort. Nobody would dream of saying that a discussion of the physiological apomorphies of our species amounted to a claim of absolute human uniqueness, so why do so when the word "behavioral" is substituted for "physiological"? Of course, there are countless ways in which our behavior closely resembles that of other species and is motivated by similar causes, as sociobiologists have been at pains to point out. And that is indeed part of the problem on which this book is intended to shed a little light.

For a consequence of its main theme is precisely that we are *not* unique in most of the ways in which we have been made out to be unique. That is, we do *not* come equipped with wisdom, logic, vast cognitive powers, novel problem-solving capacities, immaterial minds, immortal souls, and all the other baggage that has been imputed to us at one time or another. We have language grafted onto a primate brain, and that's it. We are still animals, but this two-edged gift that has been laid upon us obliges us to live in ways no other animal could conceive of.

I still feel, however, that I owe a word of explanation to those who may have been led by the title of this book to expect some rather different topics. When sociobiologists talk of human behavior, they do not generally talk about things like thinking and consciousness, or even about things like driving, dancing, boxing, or rehearsing—human as all these activities surely are. Typically they talk about things like altruism, aggression, mating patterns, rape, or incest, things for which they can find (or claim to find) plausible analogues in the behavior of other species.

Now of course our overall behavior is driven by the same forces that drive other animals. We need to mate and breed, to feed ourselves and our families, to preserve our lives and those of close kin, to defend territory, to establish our places in dominance hierarchies—things that animals in general have to do. Naturally enough, many of the ways in which we do these things are determined by biological features that we share with other species. But some of them are not. Language puts its own spin on the ways we execute biological imperatives—a spin that is not always noticed, and seldom understood, in the sociobiological literature.

Let's look briefly at two aspects of human sexual practices, adultery and incest. It is true, of course, that "we evolved, like other animals, to win at the contest of leaving as many descendants as possible" (Diamond 1992:98). And it is also the case that, in order to maximize their success, many species, even those bird species that are habitually monogamous, practice what has been termed "adultery" (Werschel 1982, Fitch and Stuart 1984).[1] Male birds practice "adultery" in ways which suggest they are maximizing their own chances of reproducing while minimizing the chances that anyone will impregnate their mates, presumably under the genetic imperative described by Dawkins (1976). And as Diamond points out, many human practices, from chastity belts to infibulation, are aimed at achieving similar objectives.

One would expect, then, that the main motive of human adulterers would be that of spreading their seed as widely as possible. Nothing could be further from the truth. In the first place, adulterers do all in their power to *prevent* spreading their seed: being the cause of pregnancy in someone other than one's wife can lead to all kinds of unpleasant consequences (legal, social, cultural, and economic), while bearing the child of someone other than one's husband may result in anything from divorce to murder. Second, the sociobiologists' explanation of the motives behind sexual

---

1. It is surely legitimate to put "scare quotes" around terms developed originally in a solely human context when these are applied to behavior in other species. Adultery as we know it occurs within, and is defined by, codes of law and culture that have no equivalent in other species. But "extra-pair copulation," which is how zoologists generally describe such behavior in birds, doesn't have quite the punch and readership attraction of "adultery."

promiscuity are not the same as those given by professional researchers in human sexuality. According to McCary (1973:396): "In the case histories of almost all the men studied, promiscuous behavior proved to be the result of feelings of inadequacy, emotional conflicts and other personality problems." No evidence suggests that these men have a higher sex drive than others (Kirkendall 1961). On the contrary, "when seriously depressed by these feelings [of inadequacy], they seek relief in irresponsible sexual relations," in part at least because of "the traditional American attitude that associates security with love, and love with sex" (McCary 1973:406). In other words, motives for adultery in male humans derive less from any biological drive they might share with other animals and more from the interaction of culturally bound, linguistically transmitted representations of ideal states with their own concepts of self—factors unknown to other species, but highly predictable in a species driven by language.

A still grosser mismatch between sociobiological prediction and reality is found in the treatment of incest. Wilson (1978:38) has claimed that in humans, incest avoidance is "guided by an instinct based on genes." Alexander (1979:197), objecting to this, has insisted that despite its universality, and despite the fact that it contributes to inclusive fitness, "incest avoidance is socially learned." However, both writers, like many other sociobiologists, have taken at its face value the supposed "abhorrence of incest" reflected in the near universality of cultural prohibitions against it. It seems not to have occurred to them that nobody would bother to prohibit what everyone naturally abhorred (there are no such taboos against drinking urine or eating excrement, for example).

In fact, the main taboo against incest is "the taboo against talking about it" (Justice and Justice 1979:17). The real situation is that "children are at higher sexual risk in their own homes than on the streets. . . . One researcher states that 4 to 5 percent of the population is involved in incest" (pp. 14, 16). Indeed, Woodbury and Schwarz (1971) concluded that the population percentage involved could not be lower than five and could run as high as fifteen. In other words, incest abhorrence is a myth, but it is a useful myth for sociobiologists, because it is easily explicable in their terms: outbreeding is relatively more adaptive than inbreeding, and sexual behavior is about breeding, so either genetic factors (Wilson) or social learning (Alexander) *ought* to discourage incest. But since human behavior is driven to a very large extent by internal representations, sex isn't, for the most part, about breeding anymore (as we saw in the case of adultery above). Quite other factors—factors that involve concepts of self and of others that couldn't even arise in an alingual species—have long since placed their unavoidable stamp on our behavior.

There is an interesting book to be written on a language-based re-interpretation of sociobiological findings, but this isn't it. I wanted to concentrate on those areas where we have least in common with other species, and explain how those areas came to be. The idea that language is primarily responsible for those areas of difference is not, one might have thought, a particularly difficult or complex one. It is therefore somewhat discouraging to note the frequency with which this apparently very simple idea is misunderstood by some extremely intelligent minds. I'll give just one example of this, involving the late Eric Newell, who before his untimely death was a leading pioneer in the field of artificial intelligence.

Newell contributed a target article to the journal *Behavioral and Brain Sciences* (Newell 1992) concerning a model—SOAR—that would attempt to replicate and machine-instantiate human cognition (see also Newell 1990). I wrote a commentary on that article (Bickerton 1992), pointing out that language was a representational system (not a mean of com-munication or a skill, as Newell had said it was) and, as such, it was the source of peculiarly human cognition, not a consequence of it. Newell's response to that commentary is worth quoting at length: "My accep-tance of the reviewers' position stumbles a bit, however, when Bickerton maintains that, contra the treatment in *Cognition* [Newell 1990, not the journal of that name, DB], language is a representational system. Did he not read the book? The book deals fundamentally and at great depth with the cognitive architecture being a representational system, what that means, and how that is possible. Language *within such a system* is of course abidingly representational—what else could it be? Language doesn't have to be its own representational system. It participates in the representational character of the system as a whole" (Newell 1992:471–emphasis added).

I'm sorry that it's no longer possible to explain this misunderstanding to Newell himself. Given that opportunity, I would have said: Yes, I *did* read the book and I *did* appreciate that the cognitive architecture is and must be a representational system—what else could it be? But as far as I am concerned, language is *not* "within such a system"—rather the architecture of cognition, or at least that part of it that is peculiar to our species, *lies within language,* and human cognition has the properties it does have precisely because it came out of language, and not vice versa.

By language, as I hope I have made clear throughout this book, I do not mean sound waves coming out of mouths, or conventionalized marks on pages, or French, Latin, Swahili, or any of the other local manifestations of language. I am talking about the infrastructure of language: the properties and consequences of the system of neuron ensembles and connecting nerve fibers that made possible, first, the first and only symbolic system for transmitting objective information that emerged on this planet,[2] and second, the refinement of that symbolic system whose use we enjoy today. Apparently the idea that language is the hen while human cognition is the egg strikes some observers as so utterly heterodox, so counter to all responsible thinking on these issues that they fail to comprehend it, dismiss it out of hand, or conclude that I must *really* mean something else. But I do not mean anything else: I mean, quite simply and straightforwardly, that human cognition came out of language—no more and no less than that.

Those who sympathize with that point of view can take heart from the fact that the conventional wisdom on this whole topic is riddled with lacunae and inconsistencies. The conventional wisdom contends that our brains got big, and that was what gave us intelligence, consciousness, and language. But as we saw in Chapter 2, brains got even bigger than they are now without any significant changes in behavior or any unambiguous sign of intellectual increment, however slight. Moreover, the conventional view which claims that greater complexity in the brain underlies our achievements has never produced any explanation of what that complexity consists in, or of how it makes our achievements possible. Mysterious inference engines, logic modules, problem-solving devices, and other cognitive mechanisms are hypothesized but never explicated nor demonstrated; still less is there any account of how or when or why they might have arisen in the course of human evolution. The problems that would be posed by any attempt at evolutionary explanation (If these

2. With apologies to the bees. I mean, of course, the first such symbolic system that could transmit information *without limit*—or at any rate without any obvious limit imposed by the biological nature of the organism itself.

mysterious faculties arose after language, how was there time for this? If they arose before language, why is there no evidence of any trace of them in either presently related or ancestral species?) are not even confronted, let alone resolved.

If the conventional wisdom is riddled with questions for which the conventional answers are totally inadequate, perhaps it is time to abandon the conventional wisdom and start over. As I hope to have shown in this book, a view that treats language as primary and sees our particular types of intelligence and consciousness as deriving directly from our possession of language can handle all of those awkward questions, either by answering them directly or by showing them to be irrelevant. Moreover, the model of language, intelligence, consciousness, and their dependent behaviors, cognitive and other, that has been developed here entails hypotheses about the nature and mode of functioning of the human brain that should be empirically testable, especially now that increasingly sophisticated methods of brain imaging can be exploited. But even in advance of such confirmation, the explanatory power of a language-based theory of human behavior should be enough to convince the unbiased observer that only through an understanding of language will we ever understand ourselves.

Appendix A

Samples of protolanguage

1. Pidgin

Sources: (a) and (b) Roberts, unpublished data (see Roberts 1995 for relevant information), (c) Reinecke 1971.

a. Pidgin Hawaiian

Nuinui pool. Make kanaka (Much-much gun. Kill men) [1791]

Maitai, nana Amerita (Good, see America) [1791]

Apopo tabu. Aole hanahana (Tomorrow forbidden. Not work) [1809]

Maitai, nuinui maitai (Good, much-much good) [1820]

Maitai palapala hanahana (Good write work) [1820]

Aole oe makemake wahine holoi lole? (Not you want woman wash clothes) [1873]

Aole hiki noho. Aole wai mauka. Hiki no (Not can stay. Not water upwards. We can) [1876]

Pau no. Wau hele Laupahoehoe. Aole wau kuleana oe (Finish, right? I go L. Not I business you) [1889]

Nuinui pilikia. Hooku. Aole lawe halewai (Much-much trouble. Let-go. Not take jail) [1889]

Wau aole hana hou (I not do again) [1893]

Makemake kuai pihi. Pihi momona (Want buy fish. Fish fat) [1893]

Wau makemake kue pake. Hanahana *hamabaga* (I want annoy Chinese. Do humbug) [1894]

Iapana, makana *dala*. Oe hiamoe ma kela hale wau (Japanese, gift dollar. You sleep at that house I) [1894]

Aole makana dala, wau hanamake oe (Not gift dollar, I make-dead you) [1899]

Kela *ten dollars* makana au. Oe kipu au. Aole piliwaiwai (That 10 dollar gift I. You bribe I. Not gamble) [1901]

Pehea hanapaa kela *ditch* (Why close that ditch?) [1906]

Oe hele olelo. Wau pilikia nuinui (You go speak. I trouble much-much) [1906]

b. Pidgin English

Take care. By and by you dead. Tiana too many men [1791]

Me no sleep. Me look. Me speak [1819]

By and by, money *pau* (finish), all gone. Then *kanaka* work plenty [1835]

By by, me die . . . Me no see [1844]

Watee namee you? . . . Liee, namee Harry [1848]

You stop, me make one. Me go now. Come again. Dood-bye! [1880]

Me very good now. Me come here work. Lick man no good [1881]

Too much work. Too warm. Some more tomorrow. No use, *mahope* (by and by) [1891]

You go to Wailuku no time. Me fine team. Me beat 'em all [1893]

You see. I got wood there. Plenty men here no job. Come steal [1895]

Me no *sabe* (know) war. Me sabe lojikosu (washing clothes) [1897]

I no got money. I no likee fight. Suppose you likee money, you catchem boss [1897]

No can. I try hard get good ones. Before, plenty duck. Now no more [1901]

You no good man. You too much steal [1902]

Me lucky. You no *pi-mai* (come), me *make* (dead) [1903]

Me *hapai* (carry) one tub of *sake*. No *makana* (gift) dollar this time. Pay day *makana* dala. Me hapai Honolulu boss [1904]

Me no have got. Me no smoke. Me no drink. Me Christian [1907]

c. Tay Boi (Vietnamese Pidgin French)

Moi faim (I hungry) Moi tasse (My glass)

Lui aver permission repos (He have permission rest)

Demain moi retour campagne (Tomorrow I return [noun] country)

Vous pas argent mon stop travail (You not money, I stop work)

Monsieur content aller danser (Mister happy go dance?)

Lui la frapper (He there beat)

Bon pas aller (Good not go) Pas travail (no job)

Assez, pas connaitre (Enough, not know)

Moi compris tu parler (I understand you speak)

2. Child language

Sources: (a) Robert Wilson, unpublished data (see Wilson 1985 for relevant information), (b) Richard Brislin, unpublished diary data, (c)–(e) CHILDES computerized data base.

a. Seth (23 months)

Read story	Kick it?	Eat come
Put on tight	Put back	Put there
Can put it	Want dry off	Dry you
Can talk?	Want talk?	More story
Want tape-recorder	Geese say	Put clothes on
Put away	You take off	Apple juice
Go open door	Put your	Little bird
Peanut-butter jelly	refrigerator	Take off
Big kiss	More juice	Some music

b. Cheryl (23 months)

where ni-ni	bed ni-ni	see birdies
bath dog wawa	more cake	where hand and arm
want my ni-ni	where birdie	where wash
daddy walk	hold horse	nice hair
baby hot	Barbara Mark ball	mama wash ni-ni
want that	here mug	see daddy
want slide swing	mommy watch	where other shoe
duck quack-quack	want baloney	where pool
where bubble		

c. Eve (19 months)

More coffee	More grape juice too	At home
Drink juice	Eve spoon	Fraser cup
Get grape juice cup	Drink coffee	I see
Hurt self	Play those	Want nother one
Graham cracker	Open toy box	Horsie stuck
Now fix a Lassie	Now Mommy read	Want Mommy read
Cromer busy	I get paper	Drop choochoo train
I help stool	Write a pencil	Pencil table
Pretty picture	My pencil	You write a pencil
Write a pencil	That a page	More page
Fraser coffee		

d. Adam (25 months)

Play checkers	Big drum	Big horn
Alright look TV	Put dirt up	Read shadow
Adam checker	I got horn	Like it
Horse go	Mott apple juice	Take two
Daddy go?	Where go	Daddy car
There bunnyrabbit	I get that brush	My screwdriver
Hear tractor	Put truck window	Busy bulldozer
Alright see that!	What (th)at	I change diaper
Adam fall	Adam fall toy	Paper find

e. Peter (23 months)

Fix it	Turn it	Broke it
Tear up	Turn around	More tape
More doggie	Two wheels	Right there
Door shut	No more	Book box
Close it	Screw it	Make one
Take picture	More cookie	Other ones
Thumb here	New truck	Put back
Get home	Get more	Get more
Man now	I put back	Turn it over
Put them back	Take off this	No more wheels
More than that	More fix it	

3. Ape "language"

Sources: (a) Patterson 1978, (b) Gardner and Gardner 1974, (c) Green-field and Savage-Rumbaugh 1991.

a. Koko (gorilla)

That cat	That bird	Red berry
More pour	Me can't	Go bed
Me good	Hot potato	Me listen
Koko purse	Hat mine	Alligator me
Give me drink	You eat	Time milk
Open bottle	Catch me	Hurry gimme
You chase me	You tickle me	
Breakfast eat some	More cereal	
cookie eat	Sorry me	

b. Washoe (chimpanzee)

That food	That drink	Washoe sorry
Drink red	Baby mine	You hat
Give me flower	Go flower	Look out
You drink	Roger tickle	Tickle Washoe
Open blanket		

c. Kanzi (bonobo)

Bite chase	Bite you	Hide Austin
Slap you	Matata bite	Penny tickle
Chase food	Food chase	Dog go
Outdoors chase	Orange open	Trailer go
Chase bad	Bite cherry	Ball slap
Balloon you	Ice water	Give Kanzi
Peanut jelly	Peanut hamburger	Austin peanut
That apple	That raisin	Food that
Peanut trailer	No balloon	Trailer peanut
Chase bite you	Grab bite you	Chase hide you

Bibliography

Alexander, R. D. 1979. *Darwinism and human affairs*. Seattle: University of Washington Press.

Angel, L. 1989. *How to build a conscious machine*. Boulder: Westview Press.

Applewhite, P. B. 1973. Habituation in the protozoan *Spirostomum* and problems of learning. In A. Perez-Miravete, ed., *Behavior of micro-organisms*, 229–33. New York: Plenum Press.

Arbib, M. 1972. Consciousness: The secondary role of language. *Journal of Philosophy* 69:579–91.

Bellugi, U., and E. S. Klima. 1982. From gesture to sign: Deixis in a visual gestural language. In R. J. Jarvella and W. Klein, eds., *Speech, place and action: Studies of language in context*, 297–313. New York: Wiley.

Bellugi, U., A. Bihrle, H. Neville, T. L. Jernigan, and S. Doherty. 1991. Language, cognition and brain organization in a neurodevelopmental disorder. In M. Gunnar and C. Nelson, eds., *Developmental behavioral neuroscience*, 201–232. Hillsdale, NJ: Erlbaum.

Bellugi, U., P. P. Wang, and T. L. Jernigan. 1994. Williams' syndrome: an unusual neuropsychological profile. In S. Broman and J. Grafman, eds., *Atypical cognitive deficits in developmental disorders: Implications for brain function*, 23–56. Hillsdale, NJ: Erlbaum.

Bermudez-Rattoni, F., D. Forthman, M. A. Sanchez, J. L. Perez, and J. Garcia. 1988. Odor and taste aversion conditioned in anaesthetized rats. *Behavioral Neuroscience* 102:726–39.

Berwick, R. C. 1985. *The acquisition of syntactic knowledge*. Cambridge: MIT Press.

Bever, T. G., and D. I. Langendoen. 1971. The dynamic evolution of language. *Linguistic Inquiry* 2:433–63.

Bickerton, D. 1981. *Roots of language*. Ann Arbor: Karoma.

———. 1983a. Pidgin and creole languages. *Scientific American* 249 (1):116–22.

———. 1983b. The last of Clever Hans. *Behavioral and Brain Sciences* 6:141–42.

———. 1984. The language bioprogram hypothesis. *Behavioral and Brain Sciences* 7:173–221.

———. 1986. More than nature needs? A reply to Premack. *Cognition* 23:73–79.

———. 1988. Creole langues and the bioprogram. In F. J. Newmeyer, ed., *Linguistics: The Cambridge survey*, 267–84. Cambridge: Cambridge University Press.

———. 1990. *Language and species*. Chicago: University of Chicago Press.

———. 1992. A unified cognitive theory: You can't get there from here. *Behavioral and Brain Sciences* 15:437–38.

———. 1993. Putting cognitive carts before linguistic horses. *Behavioral and Brain Sciences* 16: 749–50.

Binford, L. R. 1984. *Faunal remains from Klasies River mouth*. New York: Academic Press.

Boesch, C. 1993. Aspects of transmission of tool-use in wild chimpanzees. In K. R. Gibson and T. Ingold, eds., *Tools, language and cognition in human evolution*, 171–84. Cambridge: Cambridge University Press.

Bowerman, M. 1973. *Early syntactic development*. Cambridge: Cambridge University Press.

Bradshaw, J. L. 1988. The evolution of human lateral asymmetries. *Journal of Human Evolution* 17:615–37.

Braitenberg, V., and R. P. Atwood. 1958. Morphological observations on the cerebellar cortex. *Journal of Comparative Neurology* 109:1–34.

Brown, R. 1973. *A first language: The early stages.* Cambridge: Harvard University Press.

Burd, L., and J. Kerbeshian. 1989. Hyperlexia in Prader-Willi syndrome. *Lancet* 1989(2):983–84.

Byrne, R. W., and A. Whiten, eds. 1988. *Machiavellian intelligence: Social expertise and the evolution of intellect in monkeys, apes, and humans.* Oxford: Clarendon Press.

Calvin, W. H. 1987. The brain as a Darwin machine. *Nature* 330:33–34.

———. 1989. *The cerebral symphony: Seashore reflections on the structure of consciousness.* New York: Bantam.

———. 1993. Cerebral codes and Darwinian processes emerge from hexagonal mosaics in the brain. Manuscript.

Cheney, D. L., and R. M. Seyfarth. 1990. *How monkeys see the world: Inside the mind of another species.* Chicago: University of Chicago Press.

Chomsky, N. 1962. *Cartesian linguistics.* New York: Harper and Row.

———. 1965. *Aspects of the theory of syntax.* Cambridge: MIT Press.

———. 1975. *Reflections on language.* New York: Pantheon.

———. 1981. *Lectures on government and binding.* Dordrecht: Foris.

———. 1986. *Barriers.* Cambridge: MIT Press.

———. 1993. A minimalist program for linguistic theory. In K. Hale and S. J. Keyser, eds., *The view from Building 20: Essays in linguistics in honor of Sylvain Bromberger,* 1–52. Cambridge: MIT Press.

Churchland, P. M. 1984. *Matter and consciousness: A contemporary introduction to the philosophy of mind.* Cambridge: MIT Press/Bradford Books.

Churchland, P. S. 1986. *Neurophilosophy.* Cambridge: MIT Press.

Clahsen, H. 1989. The grammatical characteristics of developmental dysphasia. *Linguistics* 27:897–920.

Cleveland, J., and C. T. Snowdon. 1982. The complex vocal repertoire of the cotton-top tamarin. *Zeitschrift für Tierpsychologie* 58:231–70.

Cowey, A., and P. Stoerig. 1992. Reflections on blindsight. In A. D. Milner and R. D. Rugg, eds., *The neuropsychology of consciousness,* 11–37. New York: Academic Press.

Cronin, H. 1992. *The ant and the peacock: Altruism and sexual selection from Darwin to today.* Cambridge and New York: Cambridge University Press.

Curtiss, S. 1977. *Genie: A psycholinguistic study of a modern-day "wild child."* New York: Academic Press.

———. 1988. Abnormal language acquisition and the modularity of language. In F. J. Newmeyer, ed., *Linguistics: The Cambridge survey,* 90–116. Cambridge: Cambridge University Press.

Damasio, A. R. 1990. Category related recognition defects as a clue to the neural substrates of language. *Trends in Neuroscience* 13:95–98.

———, and H. Damasio. 1992. Brain and language. *Scientific American* 267:88–95.

Davidson, I., and W. Noble. 1989. The archaeology of perception: Traces of depiction and language. *Current Anthropology* 30:125–55.

———. 1993. Tools and language in human evolution. In K. R. Gibson and T. Ingold, eds., *Tools, language and cognition in human evolution,* 361–88. Cambridge: Cambridge University Press.

Dawkins, R. 1976. *The selfish gene.* New York: Oxford University Press.

———. 1986. *The blind watchmaker.* New York: Norton.

———, and J. R. Krebs. 1979. Arms races between and within species. *Proceedings of the Royal Society of London,* B, 205:489–511.

Day, M. H. 1986. *Guide to fossil man.* 4th ed. London: Cassell.

Dennett, D. C. 1969. *Content and consciousness.* London: Routledge and Kegan Paul.

———. 1978. *Brainstorms: Philosophical essays on mind and psychology.* Montgomery, Vermont: Bradford Books.

———. 1987. *The intentional stance.* Cambridge: MIT Press/Bradford Books.

———. 1991. *Consciousness explained.* Boston: Little, Brown.

Diamond, J. 1992. *The third chimpanzee.* New York: HarperCollins.

Dibble, H. L. 1987. Reduction sequences in the manufacture of Mousterian implements of France. In O. Soffer, ed., *The Pleistocene Old World: Regional perspectives,* 33–44. New York: Plenum Press.

Donachie, W. D. 1979. The life cycle of *Escherichia coli.* In J. H. Parish, ed., *Developmental biology of prokaryotes,* 11–35. Berkeley: University of California Press.

Donald, M. 1991. *Origins of the modern mind.* Cambridge: Harvard University Press.

Eccles, J. C. 1990. The mind-brain problem revisited: The microsite hypothesis. In J. C. Eccles and O. Creutzfeld, eds., *The principles of design and operation of the brain,* 549–68. Berlin: Springer-Verlag.

Edelman, G. 1989. *The remembered present: A biological theory of consciousness.* New York: Basic Books.

Eldredge, N., and S. J. Gould. 1972. Punctuated equilibria: An alternative to phyletic gradualism. In T. J. M. Schopf, ed., *Models in paleobiology,* 82–115. San Francisco: Freeman, Cooper.

Falk, D. 1987. Hominid paleoneurology. *Annual Review of Anthropology* 16:13–30.

———. 1990. Brain evolution in *Homo*: The "radiator" theory. *Behavioral and Brain Sciences* 13:333–81.

———. 1992. *Braindance.* New York: Henry Holt.

———. 1993. Sex differences in visuospatial skills: Implications for hominid evolution. In K. R. Gibson and T. Ingold, eds., *Tools, language and cognition in human evolution,* 216–29. Cambridge: Cambridge University Press.

Fiez, J., S. E. Peterson, and M. E. Raichle. 1990. Impaired habit learning following cerebellar hemorrhage: A single case study. *Society of Neuroscience Abstracts* 16:287.

Fitch, J. A., and G. W. Stuart. 1984. Requirements for a mixed reproductive strategy in avian species. *American Naturalist* 124:116–26.

Fodor, J. A. 1975. *The language of thought.* New York: Crowell.

———. 1981. *Representations.* Cambridge: MIT Press.

———. 1983. *The modularity of mind.* Cambridge: MIT Press/Bradford Books.

Foley, R. 1987. *Another unique species: Patterns in human evolutionary ecology.* London: Longman Group.

Forster, K. I. 1976. Accessing the mental lexicon. In R. J. Wales and E. Walker, eds., *New approaches to language mechanisms.* Amsterdam: North Holland.

Fouts, R. S. 1983. Chimpanzee language and elephants' tails: A theoretical synthesis. In J. de Luce and H. T. Wilder, eds., *Language in primates: Perspectives and implications*, 63–75. New York: Springer-Verlag.

Gallup, G. G. 1982. Self-awareness and the emergence of mind in primates. *American Journal of Primatology* 2:237–48.

Garcia, J. 1989. Learning without memory. *Behavioral Neuroscience* 103:287–303.

———, and R. A. Koelling. 1966. Relation of cue to consequence in avoidance learning. *Psychonomic Science* 4:123–24.

Gardner, B. T., and R. A. Gardner. 1974. Comparing the early utterances of child and chimpanzee. In A. Pick, ed., *Minnesota symposium on child psychology*, Vol. 8, 3–23. Minneapolis: University of Minnesota Press.

Gardner, H. 1983. *Frames of mind*. New York: Basic Books.

Gardner, R. 1994. Are there language-regulating genes on chromosome 15? To appear in E. Callary, ed., *Studies in language origins*. In press.

Garrett, M. F. 1978. Word and sentence perception. In R. Held, H. W. Leibowitz, and H. L. Teuber, *Handbook of sensory physiology*, Vol. 8: *Perception*, 611–25. Berlin: Springer-Verlag.

Gazzaniga, M. 1985. *The social brain*. New York: Basic Books.

Gibson, I. 1989. *Federico Garcia Lorca: A life*. London: Faber and Faber.

Gibson, K. R., and T. Ingold, eds. 1993. *Tools, language and cognition in human evolution*. Cambridge: Cambridge University Press.

Goldin-Meadow, S. 1979. Structure in a manual communication system developed without a conventional language model: Language without a helping hand. In H. Whitaker and H. A. Whitaker, eds., *Studies in Neurolinguistics*, Vol. 4, 125–209. New York: Academic Press.

Gopnik, M. 1990. Feature blindness: A case study. *Language Acquisition* 1:139–64.

Greenfield, P. M., and E. S. Savage-Rumbaugh. 1990. Grammatical combination in *Pan paniscus:* Processes of learning and invention in the evolution and development of language. In S. T. Parker and K. R. Gibson, eds., *"Language" and intelligence in monkeys and apes: Comparative developmental perspectives*, 540–78. Cambridge and New York: Cambridge University Press.

———. 1991. Imitation, grammatical development, and the invention of protogrammar by an ape. In N. Krasnegor, D. M. Rumbaugh, M. Studdert-Kennedy, and D. Scheifelbusch, eds., *Biobehavioral foundations of language development*, 235–58. Hillsdale, N.J.: Lawrence Erlbaum.

Griffin, D. R. 1992. *Animal minds*. Chicago: University of Chicago Press.

Grodzinsky, Y. 1990. *Theoretical perspectives on linguistic deficits*. Cambridge: MIT Press/Bradford Books.

———, A. Pierce, and S. Marakovitz. 1991. Neuropsychological reasons for a transformational analysis of verbal passive. *Natural Language and Linguistic Theory* 9:431–53.

Haber, R. N. 1983. When is a picture worth so many words? *Behavioral and Brain Sciences* 6:147–48.

Hadamard, J. 1945. *The psychology of invention in the mathematical field*. Princeton: Princeton University Press.

Hall, R. A., Jr. 1966. *Pidgin and creole languages*. Ithaca: Cornell University Press.

Hart, J., and B. Gordon. 1992. Neural subsystems for object knowledge. *Nature* 359:60–64.

Hart, L. 1975. *How the brain works.* New York: Basic Books.

Herman, L. M., D. G. Richards, and J. P. Wolz. 1984. Comprehension of sentences by bottle-nosed dolphins. *Cognition* 16:129–219.

Herrnstein, R. J. 1988. Objects, categories and discriminative stimuli. In H. L. Roitblat, T. G. Bever, and H. S. Terrace, eds., *Animal Cognition*, 233–62. Hillsdale, N.J.: Lawrence Erlbaum Associates.

Hilgard, E. R. 1965. *The experience of hypnosis.* New York: Harcourt, Brace and World.

Hockett, C. F., and R. Ascher. 1964. The human revolution. *Current Anthropology* 5:135–68.

Hofstadter, D. R., and D. C. Dennett. 1981. *The mind's I: Fantasies and reflections on self and soul.* New York: Basic Books.

Holloway, R. 1966. Cranial capacity, neural reorganization and hominid evolution: A search for more suitable parameters. *American Anthropologist* 68:103–21.

Holm, J. 1988. *Pidgins and creoles.* New York: Cambridge University Press.

Hooker, C. A. 1975. Systematic philosophy and meta-philosophy of science: Empiricism, Popperianism and realism. *Synthese* 32:177–231.

Hubel, D. H., and T. N. Wiesel. 1962. Receptive fields, binocular interaction and functional architecture in the cat's visual cortex. *Journal of Physiology* (London) 160:106–54.

Ingvar, D. H. 1990. On ideation and "ideography." In J. C. Eccles and O. Creutzfeld, eds., *The principles of design and operation of the brain*, 433–53. Berlin: Springer-Verlag.

Jackendoff, R. 1972. *Sematic interpretation in generative grammar.* Cambridge: MIT Press.

———. 1975. On belief-contexts. *Linguistic Inquiry* 6:53–93.

———. 1976. Towards an explanatory semantic representation. *Linguistic Inquiry* 7:89–150.

———. 1977. *X-bar syntax: A study of phrase structure.* Cambridge: MIT Press.

———. 1980. Belief-contexts revisited. *Linguistic Inquiry* 11:395–414.

———. 1983. *Semantics and cognition.* Cambridge: MIT Press.

———. 1987. *Consciousness and the computational mind.* Cambridge: MIT Press.

———. 1994. *Patterns in the Mind: Language and human nature.* New York: Basic Books.

Jacob, F. 1982. *The possible and the actual.* Seattle: University of Washington Press.

James, W. 1890. *The principles of psychology.* New York: Holt.

Jaynes, J. 1976. *The origins of consciousness in the breakdown of the bicameral mind.* Boston: Houghton Mifflin.

Jerison, J. 1973. *Evolution of the brain and intelligence.* New York: Academic Press.

Jernigan, T. L., and U. Bellugi. 1990. Anomalous brain morphology on magnetic resonance images in Williams syndrome and Down syndrome. *Archives of Neurology* 47:529–33.

———, U. Bellugi, E. Sowell, S. Doherty, and J. R. Hesselink. 1993. Cerebral morphologic distinctions between Williams and Down syndromes. *Archives of Neurology* 50:186–91.

Jia, Li, and W. Huang. 1990. *The story of Peking man.* Oxford: Oxford University Press.

Johnston, W. A., and V. J. Dark. 1986. Selective attention. *Annual Review of Psychology* 37:43–75.

Justice, B., and R. Justice. 1979. *The broken taboo: Sex in the family*. New York: Human Sciences Press.

Kegl, J., and G. A. Iwata. 1989. Lenguage de Signos Nicaraguense: A pidgin sheds light on the "creole"? ASL. *Proceedings of the Fourth Annual Meeting of the Pacific Linguistics Society*. Eugene: University of Oregon.

Kirkendall, L. A. 1961. Sex drive. In A. Ellis and A. Abarbanel, eds., *The encyclopedia of sexual behavior*, 939–48. New York: Hawthorn Books.

Kohler, W. 1927. *The mentality of apes*. New York: Harcourt, Brace.

Lefebvre, C. 1986. Relexification in creole languages revisited: The case of Haitian Creole. In P. Muysken and N. Smith, eds., *Substrata and universals in creole genesis*, 279–300. Amsterdam: Benjamins.

Leiner, H. C., A. L. Leiner, and R. S. Dow. 1989. Reappraising the cerebellum: What does the hindbrain contribute to the forebrain? *Behavioral Neuroscience* 103:998–1008.

———. 1991. The human cerebro-cerebellar system: Its computing, cognitive and language skills. *Behavioural Brain Research* 44:113–28.

Lenneberg, E. H. 1967. *Biological foundations of language*. New York: Wiley.

Leonard, B., U. Bortolini, M. C. Caselli, K. K. McGregor, and L. Sabbadin. 1992. Two accounts of morphological simplicity in children with specific language impairment. *Language Acquisition* 2:151–79.

Lieberman, P. 1984. *The biology and evolution of language*. Cambridge: Harvard University Press.

———. 1991. *Uniquely human: The evolution of speech, thought, and selfless behavior*. Cambridge: Harvard University Press.

———, and E. S. Crelin. 1971. On the speech of Neanderthal man. *Linguistic Inquiry* 2:203–22.

Lightfoot, D. 1982. *The language lottery: Toward a biology of grammars*. Cambridge: MIT Press.

———. 1989. The child's trigger experience: Degree-0 learnability. *Behavioral and Brain Sciences* 12:321–75.

———. 1991. Subjacency and sex. *Language and Communication* 11:67–69.

Linden, E. 1975. *Apes, men and language*. New York: Dutton.

Liu, Z. 1985. Sequence of sediments at locality 1 in Zhoukoudian and correlation with loess stratigraphy in northern China and with the chronology of deep-sea cores. *Quaternary Research* 23:139–53.

Lumsden, C. J., and E. O. Wilson. 1983. *Promethean fire*. Cambridge: Harvard University Press.

McCary, J. L. 1973. *Human sexuality*. 2d ed. New York: Van Nostrand.

McNeill, D. 1992. Review of *Language and species*. *International Journal of Primatology* 13:575–83.

McPhail, E. 1982. *Brain and intelligence in vertebrates*. Oxford: Clarendon Press.

———. 1987. The comparative psychology of intelligence. *Behavioral and Brain Sciences* 10:645–95.

Malson, I. 1972. *Wolf children and the problem of human nature*. New York: Monthly Review Press.

Marr, D. 1982. *Vision*. San Francisco: Freeman.

Marshack, A. 1983. A code by any other name. *Behavioral and Brain Sciences* 6:151–52.

Mayr, E. 1963. *Animal species and evolution.* Cambridge: Belknap Press of Harvard University Press.

Mellars, P. 1989. Major issues in the emergence of modern humans. *Current Anthropology* 30:349–85.

Menzel, E., E. S. Savage-Rumbaugh, and J. Lawson. 1985. Chimpanzee (*Pan troglodytes*) spatial problem solving with the use of mirrors and televised equivalents of mirrors. *Journal of Comparative Psychology* 99:211–17.

Midgley, M. 1985. *Evolution as a religion.* London: Methuen.

Miles, H. L. 1983. Two way communication with apes and the origin of language. E. de Grolier, ed., *Glossogenetics: The origin and evolution of language,* 201–10. New York: Harwood Academic Publishers.

Millward, R. 1983. Needed: Some specifics for an imaginal code. *Behavioral and Brain Sciences* 6:153–54.

Milner, A. D., and M. D. Rugg, eds. 1992. *The neuropsychology of consciousness.* New York: Academic Press.

Minsky, M. 1985. *The society of mind.* New York: Simon and Schuster.

Morton, E. S., and J. Page. 1991. *Animal talk: Science and the voices of nature.* New York: Random House.

Morton, J., and K. Patterson. 1980. A new attempt at an interpretation, or an attempt at a new interpretation. In M. Coltheart, K. Patterson, and J. C. Marshall, eds., *Deep dyslexia,* 91–118. London: Routledge and Kegan Paul.

Muhlhausler, P. 1986. *Pidgin and creole linguistics.* Oxford: Blackwell.

Naatanen, R. 1992. *Attention and brain function.* Hillsdale, N.J.: Lawrence Erlbaum.

Nadeau, R. 1991. *Minds, machines and human consciousness.* Chicago: Contemporary Books.

Newmeyer, F. J. 1991. Functional explanation in linguistics and the origin of language. *Language and Communication* 11:1–28.

Newell, E. 1990. *Unified theories of cognition.* Cambridge: Harvard University Press.

———. 1992. SOAR as a unified theory of cognition: Issues and explanations. *Behavioral and Brain Sciences* 15:464–88.

Nilsson, N. 1984. *Shakey the computer.* SRI Technical Report, SRI International, Menlo Park, California.

Ojemann, G. A., and O. D. Creutzfeld. 1987. Language in humans and animals: Contribution of brain stimulation and recording. F. Plum, ed., *Handbook of physiology, Section 1: The nervous system,* Vol. 5: *Higher functions of the brain,* 675–99. Bethesda: American Physiological Society.

Passingham, R. E. 1975. Changes in the size and organisation of the brain in man and his ancestors. *Brain, Behavior and Evolution* 11:73–90.

Patterson, F. G. 1978. Language capacities of a lowland gorilla. In F. C. C. Peng, ed., *Sign language and language acquisition in man and ape,* 161–201. Boulder: Westview Press.

———, and E. Linden. 1981. *The education of Koko.* New York: Holt, Rinehart and Winston.

Penrose, R. 1989. *The emperor's new mind.* Oxford: Oxford University Press.

Pepperberg, I. M. 1987. Acquisition of the same/different concept by an African grey parrot *Psittacus erithacus. Animal Learning and Behavior* 15:423–32.

Pinker, S. 1984. *Language learnability and language development*. Cambridge: Harvard University Press.

———. 1989. *Learnability and cognition: The acquisition of argument structure*. Cambridge: MIT Press.

———. 1992. Review of *Language and species. Language* 68:375–82.

———. 1993. *The language instinct*. New York: Morrow.

———, and P. Bloom. 1990. Natural language and natural selection. *Behavioral and Brain Sciences* 13:707–84.

Posner, M. I., and M. K. Rothbart. 1992. Attentional mechanisms and conscious experience. In A. D. Milner and R. D. Rugg, eds., *The neuropsychology of consciousness*, 91–111. New York: Academic Press.

Premack, D. 1972. Language in the chimp? *Science* 172:808–22.

———. 1983. The codes of men and beasts. *Behavioral and Brain Sciences* 6:125–68.

———. 1985. Gavagai, or the future history of the animal language controversy. *Cognition* 19:207–96.

———. 1986. Pangloss to Cyrano de Bergerac: "Nonsense, it's perfect"; a reply to Bickerton. *Cognition* 23:81–88.

Quine, W. 1960. *Word and object*. New York: Wiley.

Radford, A. 1988. *Transformational syntax: A first course*. 2d ed. New York: Cambridge University Press.

Raphael, B. 1976. *The thinking computer: Mind inside matter*. San Francisco: Freeman.

Reinecke, J. K. 1971. Tay Boi: Notes on the Pidgin French spoken in Vietnam. In D. Hymes, ed., *Pidginization and creolization of languages*, 47–56. Cambridge: Cambridge University Press.

Reinhart, T. 1983. *Anaphora and semantic interpretation*. London: Croom Helm.

———. 1986. Core and periphery in the grammar of anaphora. In B. Lust, ed., *Studies in the acquisition of anaphora*, 123–50. Dordrecht: Reidel.

Ridley, M. 1993. *The red queen: Sex and the evolution of human nature*. New York: Macmillan.

Roberts, J. 1993. The transformation of Hawaiian plantation pidgin and the emergence of Hawaii Creole English. Paper presented at the Conference of the Society for Pidgin and Creole Linguistics, Amsterdam, June 10–12.

———. 1995. Pidgin Hawaiian: A sociohistorical study. *Journal of Pidgin and Creole Languages* 10.1.

Romaine, S. 1988. *Pidgin and creole languages*. London: Longman Group.

Ryle, G. 1949. *The concept of mind*. London: Hutchinson.

Sabsay, S., and K. T. Kerman. 1993. On the nature of language impairment in Down syndrome. *Topics in Language Disorders* 3:20–35.

Sacks, O. 1985. *The man who mistook his wife for a hat*. New York: Summit Books.

Sapir, E. 1921. *Language*. New York: Harcourt, Brace and World.

Saussure, F. de. 1966. *Course in general linguistics*. New York: McGraw-Hill.

Savage-Rumbaugh, E. S. 1986. *Ape language: From conditioned response to symbol*. New York: Columbia University Press.

Schusterman, R. J., and K. Krieger, 1984. California sea lions are capable of semantic comprehension. *Psychological Record* 34:3–23.

Searle, J. 1980. Minds, brains and programs. *Behavioral and Brain Sciences* 3:417–58.

———. 1982. The myth of the computer: An exchange. *New York Review of Books*, June 24, 56–57.

———. 1988. Turing the Chinese room. In T. Singh, ed., *Synthesis of science and religion: Critical essays and dialogues*. San Francisco: Bhaktivedenta Institute.

———. 1993. The problem of consciousness. *Social Research* 60:3–16.

Simpson, G. G. 1953. *The major features of evolution*. New York: Columbia University Press.

Singler, J. 1992. Nativization and pidgin/creole genesis: A reply to Bickerton. *Journal of Pidgin and Creole Languages* 7:319–34.

Smith, N., and D. Wilson. 1979. *Modern linguistics: The results of Chomsky's revolution*. Bloomington: Indiana University Press.

Snowdon, C. T. 1993. A comparative approach to language parallels. In K. R. Gibson and T. Ingold, eds., *Tools, language and cognition in human evolution*, 109–28. Cambridge: Cambridge University Press.

Stenger, V. 1988. *Not by design: The origin of the Universe*. Buffalo: Prometheus Books.

Sternberg, P. W., K. Liu, and H. M. Chamberlin. 1992. Specification of neuronal identity in *Caenorhabditis elegans*. In M. Shankland and E. R. Macagno, eds., *Determinants of neuronal identity*, 1–43. New York: Academic Press.

Terrace, H. S. 1979. *Nim*. New York: Knopf.

———, L. A. Petitto, R. J. Sanders, and T. G. Bever. 1979. Can an ape create a sentence? *Science* 206:891–902.

Tobias, P. V. 1964. The Olduvai bed hominine with special reference to its cranial capacity. *Nature* 202:3–4.

———. 1971. *The brain in hominid evolution*. New York: Columbia University Press.

———. 1987. The brain of *Homo habilis*: A new level of organisation in cerebral evolution. *Journal of Human Evolution* 16:741–61.

Turing, A. 1950. Computing machinery and intelligence. *Mind* 59:433–60.

Tyler, L. K. 1988. Spoken language comprehension in a fluent aphasic patient. *Cognitive Neuropsychology* 5:375–400.

———. 1992. The distinction between implicit and explicit language function: Evidence from aphasia. In A. D. Milner and M. D. Rugg, eds., *The neuropsychology of consciousness*, 159–78. New York: Academic Press.

———, and H. Cobb. 1987. Processing bound grammatical morphemes in context: The case of an aphasic patient. *Language and cognitive processes* 2:245–63.

Van Valen, L. 1973. A new evolutionary law. *Evolutionary Theory* 1:1–30.

Vermeij, G. 1987. *Evolution and escalation: An ecological history of life*. Princeton: Princeton University Press.

von Frisch, K. 1967. *The dance language and orientation of bees*. Cambridge: Harvard University Press.

Wang, P. P., S. Doherty, J. R. Hesselink, and U. Bellugi. 1992. Callosal morphology concurs with neurobehavioral and neuropathological findings in two neurodevelopmental disorders. *Archives of Neurology* 49:407–11.

Washburn, S. L. 1960. Tools and evolution. *Scientific American* 203:63–75.

Weiskrantz, L. 1986. *Blindsight: A case study and implications*. Oxford: Clarendon Press.

Wernick, W. A., and S. A. Daniel. 1970. Two kinds of response priming in tachistoscopic recognition. *Journal of Experimental Psychology* 84:74–81.

Werschel, D. F. 1982. Nesting ecology of the Little Blue Heron: Promiscuous behavior. *Condor* 84:381–84.

Whinnom, K. 1971. Linguistic hybridization and the "special case" of pidgins and creoles. In D. Hymes, ed., *Pidginization and creolization of languages*, 91–115. Cambridge: Cambridge University Press.

Whiten, A., and R. W. Byrne. 1988. Tactical deception in primates. *Behavioral and Brain Sciences* 11:233–73.

Whorf, B. L. 1956. *Language, thought and reality*. Cambridge: MIT Press.

Wills, C. 1993 *The runaway brain: The evolution of human uniqueness*. New York: Basic Books.

Wilson, A. C. 1991. From molecular evolution to body and brain evolution. In J. Campisi, D. D. Cunningham, M. Inouye, and M. Riley, eds., *Perspectives on cellular regulation: From bacteria to cancer*, 331–40. New York: Wiley-Liss, Inc.

Wilson, E. O. 1972. Animal communication. In W. S-Y. Wang, ed., *The emergence of language: Development and evolution*, 3–15. New York: Freeman & Co.

———. 1975. *Sociobiology: The new synthesis*. Cambridge: Harvard University Press.

———. 1978. *On human nature*. Cambridge: Harvard University Press.

———. 1992. *The diversity of life*. Cambridge: Harvard University Press.

Wilson, R. 1985. The emergence of markers of tense and aspect in the development of a visually-impaired child. Ph.D. dissertation, University of Hawaii.

Winograd, T. 1972. *Understanding natural language*. New York: Academic Press.

Woodbury, J., and E. Schwarz. 1971. *The silent sin: A case history of incest*. New York: Signet Books.

Young, J. Z. 1978. *Programs of the brain*. Oxford: Oxford University Press.

Index